KISSING THE FACE OF GOD

Worship That Changes the World

Dale Walker

www.xulonpress.com

CONTENTS

ACKNOWLEDGMENTS

I t has been a joy working on this manuscript and being able to tell some adventures of worship and compassion. I want to thank the many people who have made it possible to complete this book: my wife, Sharon, and our children for being outrageously kind and supportive in this journey; my parents, Fred and Eileen Walker, who taught me to have God's heart for the world; my natural brothers and sisters – Jerry, Beverly, Steve, Janey, and Tommy – and their spouses, who, as you will read, have walked this journey and inspired me; and the Heart for the World staff, who are carrying out this dream. I particularly want to thank Pat, Lydia, and Rhonda for the tireless hours they have worked to edit and help me prepare this manuscript. And I want to thank the Heart for the World Church congregation, who are such a joy and treasure in my life. Of course, I thank You, Jesus, because whatever has happened to give God glory, it was all Your work.

ENDORSEMENTS

Kissing the Face of God has literally changed my concept of what worship is and the unexpectedly powerful ways God can flow through it! A must-read for every worship leader, missionary, and pastor.
– Tommy Walker, Worship Leader; Song Writer; Recording Artist; Author

This book depicts the amazing and essential solidarity between worship and compassion. Dale's selfless abandonment to worship will serve as a catalyst to extract, resurrect, and develop your latent gift of compassion (mercy in action) and prepare you for a new level of creative expression and service. His revelation of worship is captured from varied experiences and comes through clearly. Investment in reading this book will be for you a defining moment.
– Delane Bailey-Herd, Project Manager, Food for the Poor, Haiti

In *Kissing the Face of God,* Dale Walker offers a refreshing view of compassion and worship entwined as one – into an unstoppable experience of intimacy with God and a limitless supply of energy to go where He sends us. This compelling account – always honest, often humorous –highlights God's triumphant rescue of seemingly hopeless efforts. With heart-zapping words, Walker inspires us to drink deeply from the well of worship, where we find an endless supply of compassion to share, showing that God blesses what we let go of.

– A reader in Las Cruces, New Mexico

INTRODUCTION

"You shall love the Lord your God with all your heart, with all your soul, and with all your mind." (Matt. 22:37, NKJV)

God does extraordinary things when we live a life of compassion given as an expression of worship. That's what this book is about – the way worship and compassion work together – and the way they were always meant to work together. After all, worship without compassion leads to empty ritualism, while compassion without worship leads to burnout. But worship *with* compassion leads to maximum impact.

God wants us to drink the new wine of His Spirit, and then pour out the oil of compassion on a broken world. He wants us to inhale His presence in worship, and then exhale His presence in acts of love and compassion. Didn't Jesus say the great commandment is both to love the Lord your God with all of your heart and to love your neighbor as yourself? Passion in God and compassion for people are two sides of the same coin, like two blades of the same scissors working together to honor God and point the way for His Kingdom to come and His will to be done on earth.

What *is* the greatest, over-the-top worship experience available today? I believe it is a worship that expresses the deepest love we can give vertically to God, and at the same time, overflows in authentic compassion to the lost, the last, and the least. Both touch the Father's heart. Both break chains of darkness. Both bring His manifest presence to sad hearts.

Over the past several years, I have had the privilege of traveling many places around the world. I have been to remote parts of Africa, Asia, and Latin America, spending time with the poorest of the poor and some of the most forgotten people in the world: street kids; AIDS patients; orphans; widows; and victims of violence, famine, and drought. What has surprised me the most has *not* been the sorrow – that was expected – but the joy that I have seen and the joy I have experienced wherever worship and compassion have flowed together. I have seen how compassion *completes* worship by making God's love practical and tangible. I have seen worship lift the hearts of poor and hurting people to see beyond their suffering, to find life-changing hope in the eyes of a heavenly Father whom they discover is looking back on them, telling them they are favored, loved, and on Heaven's "most wanted" list.

What happens first in worship? In worship, we experience God – we know Him in His fullness. We expose our spirit to who He is and to who we are in

His presence. In worship, as we abandon ourselves to Him, we receive His acceptance. It's a two-way relationship – He breathes into us as we adore Him. What He desires most is our affection, so we don't just "have" God – we pursue Him madly: we pursue a first-love relationship with Him. As David said, "My soul thirsts for You, my flesh longs for You in a dry and weary land" (Ps. 63:1, NASB).

In true worship, we can be real with God: honest, vulnerable, spontaneous. We are not out to impress Him. And it is in this mutual longing – God for us and us for Him – that we enter a zone of access. Once we prepare an environment in our hearts, He will come. In worship, we empty out as we yield – and He fills us. The more we worship, the more we feel His love flow through us, healing and trans- forming us. Worship helps us know how loved we are by Him, how approachable He is – how near. And always we want to remember the cost of this inti- macy in worship – to appreciate the sacrifice of Jesus on the cross. We want to worship Him as extrava- gant "vase-breakers"—with an attitude of passionate expectancy.

We aren't born compassionate – I was not a com- passionate person until I found Jesus. It was then that I saw hungry people and began to weep.

Unfortunately, many of us, though we know Christ and have seen our own capacity for compas- sion grow, have become burdened – burnt out – by *compassion fatigue*. Similarly, though we long to stay fresh and passionate in our worship, we have lost the sense of our first love in worship, and of our need for constant renewal. We have lost the refueling presence of the Holy Spirit and replaced the Lord of work with the work of the Lord, and we no longer see that we are ministering to Jesus in others.

Instead of worship and compassion being expressions of each other, they have become separate acts; instead of feeding and strengthening each other through the power of the Holy Spirit, worship and compassion have dried up. We have forgotten that true worship, true compassion, do not come from our human sincerity, or even from our human effort. True worship and true compassion are *unctions of grace* –the impartation of the Holy Spirit that He brings as we give worship and compassion as expressions of each other.

The heart message of this book is to share how both worship and compassion can be revitalized in our lives as we understand the way God intends them to be linked:

Worship provides fuel for compassion. Worship causes love to replace duty in our service to Christ. It transforms earthly actions into heavenly deeds. It unleashes divine grace through simple acts of servanthood. *Compassion* makes our words real and authentic. Compassion insures that our worship is practical, not just poetic; it is from the heart and not just the head. Compassion makes worship complete by adding works to words, demonstration to explanation. It is the proof that, somewhere in our worship, what is in the heart of God, has taken over our hearts as well.

John Wimber, who was pivotal in establishing the Vineyard movement, described what he felt were *the two legs of the Vineyard man:* worship and compassion. It is as we walk on these two legs that the kingdom of God is advanced. As a pastor, I was deeply impacted by John's teaching on these matters. And over the last thirty years, my wife Sharon and I have sought to develop a ministry based on these foundations. Our journey of worship and compassion has led us from a small church in El Paso to a global outreach and involvement beyond anything we could have imagined. Today I am both senior pastor of Heart for the World Church in Las Cruces, New Mexico, and Director of Heart for the World Ministries, an interdenominational mission ministry made up of churches, businesses, and individuals, reaching out to share the love of Jesus Christ with the nations of the world.

This book is a collection of the insights we have gained from this journey. Our purpose is to help you discover the fullness of worship that God has for you – worship that reaches its fullest expression in acts of compassion – while at the same time to help you develop a life of compassion that is centered in a life of worship. I believe that both worship and compassion are one in the heart of God and both find their fullest expression in combination.

About This Book

ﻋﻠﻰ

Organizing these reflections was an interesting process: God has blessed our experience of worship and compassion in a multi-faceted way – with outcomes that were rich, diverse, and unpredictable. We can see worship and compassion, when inseparably linked, like a prism that God shines His light through. In the same way light through a prism splashes us with striking colors, God, through our worship and compassion, reflects on us His love and truth in ways that are startling, beautiful, yet uncontainable.

In the first chapter of this book, "The Fullness of Worship," I explore the surprising way God meets us when we show up: how he guides us into authentic worship; into keeping our lamps filled; and finally, into seeking His presence in the crushed in spirit, the hopeless ones, the "least of these."

In the second, third, and fourth chapters, I continue to explore finding Jesus in the least of these, as we take worship and compassion into the darkest corners of the earth: how in giving our best to the undesirables, the antagonistic, and to the children of the poor and the oppressed, *we* receive favor. And as we chase Jesus to where He is looking, we find His presence powerfully in the suffering and the hurt ones – and we experience Him as never before.

In the fifth chapter, "Global Compassion," the focus is on going global: showing the increase in faith and miracles as we stay weak and broken (and still He fills us). What we let go of as individuals, and as a church, God multiplies beyond all expectation.

Questions for discussion are included at the end of each chapter. Also included at the end of the text are additional questions, journaling exercises, a checklist for obstacles to worship and compassion, a list of things to do, and a recommended reading list.

If you feel dry in either your worship or compassion, my hope is this book will shed new light on our deepest desires: to adore God and to be near Him in an intimate way, and at the same time, to serve others, especially those who need us the most.

CHAPTER ONE

THE FULLNESS OF WORSHIP

عل

Kissing the Face of God

True worship leads us to live beyond ourselves in acts of compassion. These acts become an offering to other people of the undeserved mercy that God has lavished upon us. Some have even described a ministry of compassion as a discovery of Jesus sacramentally present in the poor in a similar way that He is present in communion. It is a mystery that cannot be fully explained but only discovered and experienced. Often, the presence of Christ is deepest and strongest among the people and in the situations where we are the least comfortable:

> *"Lord, when did we see You hungry and feed*
> *You, or thirsty and give you drink? When did*
> *we see You a stranger and take You in, or*

naked and clothe You? Or when did we see
You sick, or in prison, and come to You?"
And the King will answer and say to them,
"Assuredly, I say to you, inasmuch as you did
it to one of the least of these My brethren, you
did it to Me." (Matt. 25:33-40, NKJV)

Saint Francis discovered this. He was terrified by the disease leprosy. One day, he was confronted on the road by a man with leprosy. As he was preparing to move quickly to the other side of the road, he heard the Lord telling him to embrace and kiss the man. He was terrified and undone by the command. But as he obeyed and kissed the man, his life was changed and his destiny was set. He turned to walk away, and as he looked back, the man had disappeared. He knew then that he had just kissed Jesus.

Every act of compassion creates space for the Kingdom of God to come – when we reach out, God shows up.

One December at a prayer meeting, we had felt the Lord lead us to pray for the "hidden ones," those who suffer outside the view of caring people. We prayed for shut-ins, bedridden and handicapped people, prisoners, mental patients, and of course, the elderly. And we prayed for those who took care of them. We felt the Lord say that if we would ask, He would show us those who were struggling the most, but had no one, or very few, who cared about them. We were particularly drawn to one nursing home on the outskirts of Las Cruces, New Mexico – a home especially for those completely dependent on social security and Medicare. These residents would certainly fit into the category of the poor Jesus described in Matthew 25.

There seemed to be a bleakness in the cold air, clouds, and wind, as we drove up to the nursing home that December day. The dreariness on the outside was matched by the dreariness on the inside as we entered with a small, but enthusiastic team of worshipers from our church. We had come to sing Christmas carols and lift the hearts of the patients with a time of worship and fellowship. This nursing home was definitely not like the one near the country club: we were where those who couldn't afford the nicer homes, and who had no other place to go, were sent.

As we entered the room of elderly people – mostly Alzheimer's patients in wheelchairs, many in the advanced stages of the disease – I couldn't help but notice the stale and unpleasant smells in the room, and the depressed spirits of the patients. Most of them were slumped over in their chairs, asleep. I later found out many had been all but abandoned. But the attendants were kind and friendly, and before you knew it, we had a group of thirty or so people in wheelchairs circled around us.

We tried to be as enthusiastic as we could. I picked up my guitar, and we started singing "Joy to the World." I had my eyes closed and thought we were sounding really good, and that surely these dear elderly people were going to be blessed by our tremendous performance. As the song concluded, and

I opened my eyes, I saw the whole group, heads down in an even deeper sleep. The only applause we received was a chorus of snoring.

I decided to try my best sermon on them. With force and power, I preached the uncompromising Word. It seemed all of them made a decision that afternoon: the decision to stay asleep. I thought to myself, "Walker, you've lost your anointing." But just then, I had what I think was a *God-thought:* "Just go kiss each one on the forehead, and tell them, *I love you.*"

I went to the first one. "I love you!" I whispered as I gently kissed this elderly gentleman's forehead. "Snoooooooooore" was his response. I went to the next and the next; still the same response. Finally, I came to an elderly woman who seemed especially unresponsive. I bent over and kissed her forehead as kindly as I could. "I love you," I said.

Suddenly, she bolted up, threw her arms around me, and squealed, "Oh, I love you, too!" From that moment on, the mood in the room changed – it came *alive.* Other team members began receiving warm responses. God's presence filled the room that day. We laughed together, gave out candy canes and little presents, listened to stories, and enjoyed how most of them tried to sing Christmas carols with us. And they let us pretend to dance with them in their wheelchairs.

The nurses thanked us profusely for making their day, for what we had shared. And as we were leaving, all of us felt such a profound sense of God's joy and presence. Later, I told the team what I felt God was saying to us as we left: "Thank you. I was so lonely today, so empty, and so afraid – missing my family so. But you came, you loved me, and your kisses and hugs calmed my heart. I had felt forgotten, but now I know I am loved. Thank you."

As I shared this with the team, I remember a kind of shudder inside as the thought gripped me: "Oh my, I just kissed the face of God."

Authentic Worship

Have you ever noticed how intense the Old Testament prophets were in addressing the shallowness and hypocrisy of the people? There was certainly never any subtlety in their messages. If you had bad breath, they were *not* the kind of guys who would say "How about a tic tac®?" They were much more likely to just come out and say, "Your breath stinks!"

I believe the reason the Old Testament prophets were so blunt was their passion for authenticity. They couldn't mince words because they truly understood that hypocrisy kills, and that denial is deadly. Even today, the greatest danger to the advancement of the Kingdom of God – and the spiritual health of God's people – could be superficial, inauthentic *church- ianity:* a type of lifeless religiosity. If our worship isn't real, our ministry can't be relevant. If it isn't authentic, it can't be anointed. And if it isn't anointed, lives won't be changed.

Evangelist Juan Carlos Ortiz talks about how people responded when TVs were first introduced in Argentina. They were status symbols. Few could afford TVs, but hundreds reached out to buy antennas to put on their houses so the people who lived in them could look important.

It is so easy for us to slip into the *going-through-the-motions* mode – of just words and actions on the outside, but without a life-giving, spirit-to-spirit encounter on the inside. The truth is that it is possible for all of us to allow our worship to sink to such lows. One of the most dangerous places we can be is in a place where we look, sound, and appear great on the outside, while our soul is cold and shrinking on the inside. The truth is most of us could admit we have been there. We have had the form of worship but lacked the power thereof. Or we go on with meeting after meeting, but very little change or transformation occurs. We impress people but grieve the Holy Spirit.

Isaiah the prophet laid the ax to the root of the hypocrisy which was such a problem in the church of his day: "I have had enough of your burnt offerings; don't bring me any more futile sacrifices, your incense are an abomination to me. Wash yourselves clean; put away the evil of your doings from before My eyes. Cease to do evil, learn to do good. Seek justice. Rebuke the oppressor, defend the fatherless; plead for the widow" (Isa. 1:11, 13, 16-17, NKJV).

Isaiah offers a road map back to spiritual authenticity in worship. He gives three steps back:

The first step is to get *real* and come clean about the offenses, impurities, and insincerity in your heart. David said what God desires first in worship are "the sacrifices of…a broken and contrite heart" (Ps.

51:17). Authentic worship comes when we unveil our hearts before God and invite Him into every part of our thoughts, motives, desires, and actions – we call our hearts to a lifestyle of accountability before Him in these areas. What is amazing is that to the degree we are honest and real, He is eager to lavish His grace to change, restore, and re-ignite authentic intimacy with Him. The prophet says wash and make yourself clean:

Though your sins are like scarlet,
They shall be white as snow;
Though they be red like crimson,
They shall be as wool. (Isa. 1:18, NKJV)

The second step he calls for is the pursuit of honest, personal obedience before the Lord. True worship is continually asking the Lord honestly: *How can I be personally more obedient to You in every area of life? Where is my life out of synch with You? What do I need to do to get back on track?* Isaiah says we need to be both willing and obedient as God shows us things we need to adjust in our lives.

The third step in this passage teaches us that our worship becomes authentic and refined through seeking compassion and justice – a passion for authenticity in worship will drive us beyond a worship that is only in word, to a worship that is also truly in deed.

Hundreds of years after Isaiah's time, James echoed this thought when he wrote about pure religion: "Religion that God our Father accepts as pure and faultless is this: to look after orphans and widows in their distress and to keep oneself from being polluted by the world" (James 1:27, NIV). When confronting the Pharisees and lawyers, Jesus dealt with the same problem. He said, externally you display your devotion: "you tithe mint and rue and all manner of herbs, and pass by justice and the love of God" (Luke 11:42, NKJV). He described this as cleaning the outside of the cup while the inside remained full of greed and wickedness (Luke 11:39). This was one of the major indictments Jesus made – of Pharisees who would demonstrate devotion to God without compassion for people.

Our worship begins in our gathering before the Lord. It is completed in our scattering to represent the Lord to those who need comfort, care, and justice. And as we purify our worship, we discover it is measured, not by its impact on us, but by its impact on God.

I'll never forget the worship lesson learned years ago through a compassion-encounter with a precious woman from our first church. Marilyn was an elderly widow who suffered from some symptoms of dementia, but was still quite aware and vocal about her love for Jesus. She loved to worship, and she loved her pastor: me. She would sit in the front row and shout while I preached and sometimes preach my sermon back to me. She looked forward to the end of the service when I walked off the stage and she would have the chance to hug me, and tell me stories of her life. Sometimes this turned into a pretty long ordeal as she told me the same stories over and over.

One Sunday I had some plans right after church. So, as I was preaching, I was mentally preparing a quick getaway right after the closing prayer, to avoid the long conversation. I had it all planned out. That morning it was obvious that Marilyn wasn't feeling well. She had a cold and had been sneezing a lot during the sermon.

As I was closing in prayer, I was gradually moving towards the opposite edge of the stage away from Marilyn. I said, "Amen," and dismissed the service, but before I could take one step off the stage, I could hear her shouting above the crowd, "Pastor Dale, Pastor Dale, I'm over here." She was so sure I'd be looking for her that I felt I had no choice but to go and talk with her. It seemed like the time was longer than usual. She wanted prayer. We held hands, and just that second, her nose started to run, so she lifted my arm and wiped her nose on my shirt sleeve. I grimaced at first and then had to laugh, at what I *now saw* was what the Lord had thought of my ideas for a quick exit.

As I listened to her stories, and then hugged her, her eyes sparkled. Even in her stories, she was giving more thanks to God. At that moment, I felt the presence of God more than at any point in the entire service. I felt the favor of God upon her and more of the favor of God upon me.

It was as though in that moment, I could hear God saying to me, "Now your worship is complete. Now it is relevant. Now it is fully anointed and God-breathed, because it has been given not only in word, but also in deed."

Grace-Motivated Giving

Worship and compassion inspire extravagant generosity – generosity motivated by grace, not guilt – a kind of giving to the poor and needy that flows out of joyful gratitude to God for all that He has done in our lives. It is a natural response to a life of intimate fellowship with our "over-the-top, generous God," a God who delights Himself eternally in the joy of giving away all that He has and is.

Maybe you can relate to how I felt while attending a particular missions conference. The speaker was dramatically highlighting the needs of the poor, but his presentation was stinging in its criticism of our American wealth and affluence. Instead of feeling motivated or inspired to make a difference in the lives of the poor, I walked away feeling more ashamed of the nice things I had in America.

Often, many Christians avoid facing the desperate needs of the poor around the world because they are overwhelmed by the load of responsibility they are already carrying. Many times we feel we can't afford to add to our "Christian guilt load." The last thing we need is one more helping of guilt, one more thing to add to our sense of failure. This approach of guilt-induced giving is tragic because it contradicts the God-inspired motive for giving He wants to pour into our hearts: a passion for the poor and broken, not out of guilt, but from an overflowing *gratitude*.

The emphasis of the Bible is not on how much we owe God, but on how extravagantly generous God has been in choosing to love us in spite of our sinful selves. God is the source of every good and perfect gift, and He never wants us to feel guilty and unworthy in return (James 1:5, 17). Rather, He longs to impart, through our gratitude, the same heart of generosity that He has.

God is a giver who, in the words of our African brothers, loves to give "plenty too much!" And when Christians really come into an understanding of the grace of God, their giving doesn't need to be motivated through guilt. They will simply give. They just won't be able to help it, because they will discover God's own generous nature overflowing inside of them.

Paul tells the story of some Christians in Macedonia who begged for the opportunity to give to the poor, even though they had little themselves: "Now I want you to know, dear brothers and sisters, what God in his kindness has done through the churches in Macedonia. They are being tested by many troubles, and they are very poor. But they are also filled with abundant joy, which has overflowed in rich generosity" (2 Cor. 8:1-2, NLT).

Their generosity came from the *overflowing joy* of knowing that Jesus Christ, even "though he was rich, yet for your sakes he became poor, so that you through his poverty might become rich" (2 Cor. 8:9, NIV). They "excelled in this grace of giving" (2 Cor. 8:7, NIV) because they had excelled in realizing and receiving the grace of God in their worship.

I love the story of a grace-motivated giver, told in Luke 7 (verses 36-50). Here we learn the story of a sinful woman, who crashed a party that had been put on for Jesus by some of the religious elite of his day. She came rushing in with her alabaster vase of costly perfume – perfume so costly as to be equal in value to a whole year's wages. She broke the alabaster vase and poured the oil on Jesus. Then she fell at His feet, and began pouring out her tears of worship on His feet.

While the Pharisees were scandalized, Jesus was delighted. In fact, He later said that her worship would go down in worship history, as one of the purest examples of worship there is. Why? Because her giving flowed out of an overwhelming sense of gratitude. She had been forgiven much, therefore she loved much. All true service to others, all authentic expressions of compassion and justice, are expressions of this kind of worship and love for Jesus Christ.

I remember hearing the story of a missionary caring for dying AIDS patients in a dingy, dilapidated clinic in South Africa. Some friends from America visited her, and one of the visitors remarked, "I wouldn't do what you're doing for a million dollars." She replied, "Neither would I. But I would do it for Jesus, for nothing, because of what He did for me!"

This heart of worship for Jesus turns even the most costly sacrifices for others into expressions of unstoppable joy. It is not that we are really doing something *for* Jesus, but *with* Jesus, and to *honor*

Jesus in the celebration of who He is. His joy never stops flowing when we are motivated this way.

There is a beautiful passage of scripture describing what the Holy Spirit can do so powerfully in worship. A veil lies over the hearts of those unable to see the grace of God and the new covenant. When they turn to the Lord, the veil is taken away.

But whenever anyone turns to the Lord, the veil is taken away. Now the Lord is the Spirit, and where the Spirit of the Lord is, there is freedom. And we, who with unveiled faces all reflect the Lord's glory, are being transformed into his likeness with ever-increasing glory, which comes from the Lord, who is the Spirit. (2 Cor. 3:16-18, NIV)

Amy was a nineteen-year-old girl in Davao City, Philippines. She had been abandoned by her boyfriend and family, and was caring for her critically ill, hydrocephalic, newborn baby. She came to the Heart for the World Healing House in Davao, simply looking for food and help. The Healing House is an outreach house for homeless girls and boys, and those serving in the house insisted that she come and stay with them. For the next several months, as Amy took her child back and forth to the hospital, the staff and other youth in the house just loved her and helped her, and they freely gave of their resources to help cover the mounting medical costs.

One day, overwhelmed by the love of Jesus expressed through the Healing House staff and residents, Amy gave her heart completely to Jesus Christ. She fell madly in love with Him and wanted to serve Him in whatever way she could. Sadly, her baby eventually died. And though her heart was broken, she walked closely with Jesus and with her new spiritual family through her grief. Soon after this, the need arose for someone to lead a Healing House specifically for girls. Amy was clearly the one called to do this. In her role as leader of this house for girls needing help and healing, she continually gives of herself sacrificially, night and day. But the most amazing thing is that joy is continually overflowing in her life. Amy has discovered the secret joy of worship and compassion.

In worship the veil of lies that often represses the true dignity of the poor can be removed. These lies – *you have no future; you have nothing to contribute; you are inferior; you have no way out of misery, no purpose* – are stripped away by the power of the Holy Spirit in true worship. So often in worship people see their true selves for the first time in the mirror of the Father's love for them.

Compassion and love work alongside worship to confirm this truth at the deepest level. The restoration of the human soul so often comes with the revelation of the riches of God's grace and the amazing access into God's love – that allows the poor to say "I am rich" and the weak to say "I am strong" – because of what the Lord has done for us. I've found in serving among the poor how the simplest things can turn into prophetic acts of restoration.

Worship – The Oil of Compassion

Compassion is the oil that we obtain from a life of worship and personal intimacy with God. In Matthew 25, Jesus tells a parable about ten virgins – five foolish and five wise:

> *At that time the kingdom of heaven will be like ten virgins who took their lamps and went out to meet the bridegroom. The foolish ones took their lamps but did not take any oil with them. The wise, however, took oil in jars along with their lamps…. At midnight the cry rang out: "Here's the bridegroom! Come out to meet him!" The foolish ones said to the wise, "Give us some of your oil; our lamps are going out." "No," they replied, "there may not be enough for both us and you. Instead, go to those who sell oil and buy some for your selves." But while they were on their way to buy the oil, the bridegroom arrived. The virgins who were ready went in with him to the wedding banquet. And the door was shut….*
> (Matt. 25: 1-13, NIV)

This parable illustrates the importance of staying filled with the Holy Spirit's renewing and refueling presence. Fresh oil comes from a fresh intimacy with the Lord. We will not be consistently loving and compassionate if we are not overflowing with Holy Spirit reality in our inner being. And just as the Israelites had to gather manna daily, we must connect deeply and personally with the Lord on a daily basis if we are going to continue in fresh ministry to others.

The great commandment teaches us that our first responsibility is to be lovers of God so that we can be kind and loving to others. We are to be "lovers of God who work, not workers who love God." Workers who remain compassionate, gentle, sincere, and kind in spite of the challenges of living in a harsh, demanding, unkind, ungrateful culture have found the secret of "the one thing."

It was the "one thing" that Mary saw and Martha missed: being completely absorbed with Jesus, of allowing Him to be first and foremost, preeminent; being a person with a single eye, serving for an audience of One, for the glory of One.

It is the one thing that Jesus called the Ephesian church back to in Revelation 2:4 – the one thing David chased after all of the days of his life (Ps. 27:4); the one thing for which Paul forsook all, and considered all else as loss or rubbish. It is that first love, in His presence, of knowing and delighting in God Himself.

One of the subtle temptations for Christian workers is to substitute the adrenalin rush of working *for* God, for the joy of just *having* His sheer presence in our life. It is only when we are absorbed in Jesus, delighting in Him, that we will have the joy of the Lord, which is our strength. It is easy to move from one ministry experience to another, becoming satisfied with the joy of being used by God and helping others. As wonderful as it is, it is not enough to sustain us in the long journey of giving out to others over a life time. We are doing so many noble works, but we have forgotten the main thing. We have substituted the work of the Lord, for the Lord of the work. We have lost our first love.

I think this is the primary reason research shows increasing numbers of pastors leaving full-time ministry. The only joy that will sustain your strength to the end of the race is the joy of knowing Him, being lost in His presence, overwhelmed by the sense of His smile, and the warmth of His embrace. This only comes through extended times of intimacy, worship, and communion in His presence.

As stated in the Introduction, worship without compassion leads to empty ritualism, and compassion without worship leads to burnout. However, giving compassion as an act of worship leads to maximum impact.

In our church we hosted what we called Community Helps. As a gift to our community, we would offer a warm meal, clothes, free medical and legal help, as well as spiritual counseling. However, over time I noticed that the incredible joy that was present among our workers at first began to wane. Though many of the people were a delight to serve, some whom we encountered were ungrateful, rude, and even quite disturbing. I remember one gentleman whom some of the workers gently described as "creepy." He came for months with continually bigger requests and inappropriate language. Later, we learned that he had been arrested for stealing the clothes off of a corpse in a funeral home. Interactions with people like him and others were producing a major "joy drain," causing our team to feel weary, discouraged, and burned out.

As we became aware of this, the Lord led us into a night of worship in which He reminded us to focus, and to re-focus, on the One whom we were serving. God was asking us to quit looking at people, and to remember how wonderful and gracious He was. We were called to remember to Whom we were ministering. We were called to remember that we were ministering to Jesus in the poor, and not just to the poor themselves. As we did this, we felt the oil filling our lamps once again, and our service continued with the joy of His presence.

The God of the Hopeless Ones

A lawyer, who came back from a recent missionary assignment in Rwanda, shared an interesting experience. He had been there trying to help win justice for the many families who had lost their loved ones in the genocide of 1994. Part of the process included the gut-wrenching and difficult task of exhuming bodies.

In the midst of the process he asked himself why he had chosen to do this, and thought that maybe he had made a great mistake. But the Holy Spirit gently encouraged him. He said to the attorney, "You can know me by staying home and going to church. But if you want to know me in my fullness, you must go to where my presence is *focused*." The attorney knew in that moment that Jesus was there, in the Rwandan cemetery, focusing His presence on the lives of those shattered families, aching to bring justice to their lives.

Jesus said in Luke 4:18:

"The Spirit of the Lord is upon Me
Because He has anointed Me to preach good
news to the poor;
He has sent Me to heal the broken hearted,
To proclaim liberty to the captives,
And recovery of sight to the blind,
To set at liberty those who are oppressed."
(NKJV)

Many know that God wants His Spirit to be upon us. But not everyone knows why. Not everyone remembers what the Spirit of the Lord is upon us *for.* He is upon us to help us join the focus of Jesus in redeeming and restoring the poor and broken. As the Psalm says, "The LORD is close to the brokenhearted and saves those who are crushed in spirit" (Ps. 34:18, NIV). Jesus made it so clear, that the poor and the oppressed, those last on the world's list, are actually the *first* on His list. The disfavored of the world are those especially chosen for His favor. When we participate in the mission of Christ to them, we will know His presence in a way that is unlike anything else we experience on this earth.

I remember one night in Ndola, Zambia, when my brother Tommy Walker and the Christian Assembly worship band performed a concert on the dirt soccer field for the poorest of the poor. Thousands came to hear the concert and the word of God that was shared. At the invitation, a teenage girl came running forward.

She was skin and bones, the most pitiful sight I can remember seeing. She grabbed my hands. "Pastor!" she cried. "What can God do for somebody like me? I'm a prostitute. I have no home. My family has disowned me. I'm dying," she said. "Is there anything Jesus can do for me?"

At that moment, Jesus let me feel something of His pain and His compassion for this precious seventeen-year-old girl afflicted with HIV-AIDS. I shared how Jesus died for her, and wept with her as she accepted the gift of eternal life. We talked about the Heart for the World Healing House in Zambia, and spoke of the workers there who wanted to help her. I could assure her that no matter what hell she had gone through on earth, God was her Father, and Heaven and His glory would be her eternal home.

I don't know how to describe it, but I felt closer to Heaven in that moment than at any other moment I can remember in my life. It was as though I was not only *in* God's presence, I *was* His presence – His hands and His feet to a beautiful little girl being rescued out of the pit of Hell into the safe arms of Jesus.

CHAPTER ONE – QUESTIONS

1. Can you identify any blocks to intimacy in your worship?

2. Can you remember a moment when the Holy Spirit improved the dynamic in an outreach you participated in, over and above human efforts to fix things?

3. Practice searching out the "nobodies" in your everyday life that you have been oblivious to. Give them a smile or an acknowledgement, even if you don't get a response back.

4. Think of a time when you excused yourself from an opportunity to help someone with a task, or to lend an ear to a lonely person, because you were either too busy or the prospect was distasteful. How did you feel afterward?

5. Think of a kindness, a blessing, or an out-and-out rescue that you have received from God, either directly or through other people. What is one way that you can bless others with that?

6. What are some ways that you can re-charge your passion for Jesus when you are feeling burned out?

7. What is the hardest act of service you ever did? How about situations where you are serving with others today? Try worshiping together before serving and especially afterwards, to help each other remember Who is being served.

8. Are there people in your area, or perhaps even in the world, that you have felt the need to minister to, but the prospect just seemed too hopeless and unachievable? What is something that you can do today to practice getting out of your comfort zone? (You can start small if you are intimidated.)

CHAPTER TWO

CHASING JESUS

Worship Warfare

Worship is not only a wonderful blessing, but it can also be a powerful weapon to defeat injustice and evil, especially when it is combined with compassion. Through worship, not only can we *enter* into God's manifest presence, but we can *take* God's manifest presence to the darkest corners of the world.

In the Old Testament the manifest presence of God was symbolized in the Ark of the Covenant. The Israelites would take the Ark before them into battle. They would shout words such as the opening verses of Psalm 68:

May God arise, may his enemies be scattered;
may his foes flee before him.
As smoke is blown away by the wind,
may you blow them away;

as wax melts before the fire,
may the wicked perish before God.
But may the righteous be glad
and rejoice before God;
may they be happy and joyful.
Sing to God, sing praise to his name,
extol him who rides on the clouds –
his name is the LORD –
and rejoice before him.
A father to the fatherless, a defender of widows,
is God in his holy dwelling. (verses 1-5, NIV)

When the Israelites spoke words like these, the demonic powers and principalities at work in the armies of the enemies would lose their influence in the spiritual realm. As a result, the physical armies would be defeated in the natural realm.

I especially like the story in 1 Samuel 5, when the Philistines captured the Ark of the Covenant. They brought it into the temple at Ashdod and set the Ark in front of this huge ugly image of their god, Dagon. In the morning when they awoke, they were shocked to discover Dagon had fallen down in reverence to the Ark of the Covenant. They put him back in place, but the next morning, the same thing happened, except this time, his head and his hands were broken off. So the Philistines moved the Ark, but everywhere it was placed, it brought havoc to their camp. Finally they had to send it back to Israel, along with a peace offering, so that the Philistines' kingdom could recover.

The warfare of worship compassion not only tears down strongholds, it brings breakthroughs of justice and hope. The gospel writers tell the story of a paralyzed man who wanted to get to Jesus but had no access (Mark 2, Luke 5). First, he couldn't walk because he was paralyzed. Second, the crowds had so pressed in around Jesus that it seemed impossible to get to Him anyway. Impossible, that is, unless you have four friends – four friends so passionate to help you get to Jesus that they are willing to tear down a roof for you. I believe everyone needs four friends who love you so much that they are crazy enough to tear down a roof to help you get to Jesus. When these four friends removed the barriers, their friend got to Jesus and he was healed on both the inside and the outside.

Wherever you go in the developing world today, you find people trapped in cycles of poverty and systems of injustice. They will never get to the freedom Jesus has for them unless there are people like you and me to help them. People that are willing to be their friends and that are willing to go to work, creating breakthrough opportunities on their behalf.

I think it is so significant to see that our model, Jesus, didn't just preach to sinners, He became the *friend* of sinners. God doesn't call us to just give our *money* to the poor; He calls us to give *ourselves* to the poor. I like the language of Isaiah 58:10, where it says, "if you spend yourselves in behalf of the hungry and satisfy the needs of the oppressed, then

43

your light will rise in the darkness" (NIV). In other words, God is saying you are to be friends with the poor because you really need them – you need their friendship as much as they need yours. You see, God is a God of relationships, and His Kingdom is always expressed through loving relationships.

James tells us the poor are "rich in faith" (James 2:5). They can share with us the amazing wealth of finding joy in Christ, independent of living conditions and material possessions. We can share with them opportunities to help them rise in places of hope, knowledge, and stewardship. We can provide opportunities for them to become change agents and transformers of their society.

My friend, Pastor Alex Chua is one of the greatest *ceiling removers* I know. He and his team work with groups of street kids – "rugby boys and girls" – on the streets of Davao City, Philippines. *Rugby* is the brand name of an inexpensive kind of glue widely available and used to fix shoes and other things. The street children often sniff the glue to get high, as a means to help them ignore the hunger pangs they feel. Thousands of these children live on the streets of the Philippines, and most survive as pickpockets and through other illegal activities. Some of the boys in Alex's ministry have been picked up and put in jail over fifty times. I sometimes joke that I've learned to hug these kids with one hand and hold my wallet with the other.

I remember one day the Lord helped me see a picture of what He was doing through Alex and others like him, as they give their lives for these kids. I was walking the streets of downtown Davao, and a small group of rugby boys swarmed around me. As I was visiting with them and getting to know them a little bit, they began telling me how hungry they were. I decided that instead of giving them money, I would take them to the McDonald's across the street for a Happy Meal®. I quickly began to realize that the scope of what I intended to do was bigger than I had imagined. By the time I got to the door of the restaurant the number of rugby boys with me had mushroomed from six to nearly thirty. As I opened the door, we were met by a security guard with a semiautomatic rifle in his hand. He stepped between me and the boys.

"Go away from here!" he shouted in their dialect. "Get out of here now!"

I suddenly realized what these boys go through every day of their life. They hear the same things – "get out," "you're not welcome," "you're not wanted here": a life of slammed doors. I quietly whispered to the guard, "They're okay, they're with me." And I handed the guard a little love offering.

His whole disposition changed immediately, and he let the boys in. As they came in and respectfully sat down, the boys' demeanor actually seemed to change, too. It was so cool to look into their eyes and realize that the boys were walking into a whole new world they had never entered before. They stuffed down cheeseburgers and fries; they laughed and giggled with delight. They ate their Happy Meals® as *real* boys – not as rugby boys.

As I sat with them, trying to learn their names, this thought came to me: they have lived with rejection in every area of their life, beginning with their own parents. I thought, what a privilege I have just received to be able to give them access, in a very simple way, to a place of favor they could never have had access to themselves. I thought about how rich I felt, too, to have all of these amazing boys as friends.

In the next moment, I couldn't help but think that this is a picture of what happens when we who are broken and sinful are invited into the presence of God. We are suddenly in a world we could never afford to live in. What a difference we feel when we not only eat at the Lord's table but are invited into the glorious sense of being real, whole, and complete – in the presence of God.

Worship Compassion and the Favor of the Lord

Molly is the youngest of my six children. And even though she's now nineteen years old, she is, and has always been, "Daddy's girl." Molly has a special gift of knowing how to touch her Daddy's heart. I might be sitting in my study chair and she'll come up next to me and say something like, "Daddy, I'm so thankful God gave me a Daddy like you."

Sometimes I'll know a request is coming. It used to be for a trip to McDonald's, but now it's more likely for a trip to Starbucks. Even though I determine to be firm and unmoved by her request, something inside of me almost always melts and yields to her request. I think worship and compassion have a similar effect on the heart of our heavenly Father. Prayer – our intimate communion with God – and care for the poor cause His favor to be unleashed on us and on those around us.

This was the case with Cornelius:

At Caesarea there was a man named Cornelius, a centurion in what was known as the Italian Regiment. He and all his family were devout and God-fearing; he gave generously to those in need and prayed to God regularly. One day at about three in the afternoon he had a vision. He distinctly saw an angel of God, who came to him and said, "Cornelius!" Cornelius stared at him in fear. "What is it, Lord?" he asked. The angel answered, "Your prayers and gifts to the poor have come up as a memorial offering before God." (Acts 10:1-4, NIV)

Cornelius was a Gentile – someone the apostles and most of the church of that day looked upon as unclean and dangerous. Even so, his prayer and gifts for the poor caught God's attention – they had not gone unnoticed. In fact, they so stirred the heart of God that He sent an angel to Cornelius, and then an apostle (Peter), and then God brought salvation and the infilling of the Holy Spirit to Cornelius and his entire household.

Isaiah 58 is one of the great passages on worship and compassion. The prophet describes the kind of fasting God desires for us in verses 6-7: "To loose the bonds of wickedness, to undo the heavy burdens, to let the oppressed go free, and that you break every yoke."

God wants you "to share your bread with the hungry, and that you bring to your house the poor who are cast out; when you see the naked, that you cover him" (NKJV). Moreover, He doesn't want you to hide yourself from your own family (disconnecting your phone so that you don't have to take the call when your relatives need help). In verse 8, He goes on to describe the amazing favor that will come from God when you do these things:

> *Then your light shall break forth like the morning,*
> *Your healing shall spring forth speedily,*
> *And your righteousness shall go before you;*

And "the glory of the LORD shall be your rear guard" (NKJV). In other words, God will protect you from unexpected attacks.

I believe that Isaiah is saying the fast track to healing and breakthrough in your life is worship and compassion. When we give to bring God's compassion to others, it comes back to bless us in unexpected, life-transforming ways.

Sakae Konda, a precious young woman from Nagoya, Japan, experienced how bringing God's compassion to others can transform our own lives. She had suffered terribly from chronic depression for many months. She had even attempted suicide and ended up in the hospital. Sakae suffered from the worst kind of poverty: not a poverty of body but a poverty of heart and soul. Sakae was invited to join us on a short term mission trip to the Philippines. At the urging of her mother, Sakae went with us.

During her week there, she and the team stayed in the Healing House in Davao.

She participated in outreaches of love to the poor "squatter's community." Sakae played with children, served food, washed hair, sang songs, and prayed for the sick. The team noticed that by the second day she began to change. By the end of the week Sakae was completely healed and transformed. Her mother testified that she had a new daughter. In fact, since then, she has been back on other mission trips and is studying English to become a full time missionary in the Philippines. Truly, as Sakae shared her compassion with the hungry, her healing sprang forth speedily.

Heart for the World sponsors several trips to serve the poor each year. And we readily admit that it is as much for those who go and give, as it is for those who receive. *Giving* mercy is the secret to *receiving* the mercy we all need.

Releasing People to Walk in the Favor of the Lord

In Jesus' famous quote of Isaiah 61, recorded in Luke 4:18-19, He contextualizes His mission by referring to "the year of the Lord's favor."

"The Spirit of the Lord is on me, because he has anointed me to preach good news to the poor. He has sent me to proclaim freedom for the prisoners and recovery of sight for the blind, to release the oppressed, to proclaim the year of the Lord's favor." (NIV)

He was saying that His ministry would bring a fulfillment of the year of Jubilee spoken about in Leviticus 25:8-17. The year of Jubilee was an amazing concept that we are not sure was ever actually lived out by the Hebrews in the Old Testament. The idea was that every fifty years the nation was to set aside a whole year just to celebrate God. Moreover, during this year, all debts were to be cancelled; all slaves and prisoners were to be set free; and all family inheritances and properties were to be restored.

The prophet Isaiah prophetically described the mission of Messiah as the introduction to the world of the true reality of the Jubilee. He called it the year of the favor of the Lord. In the material world, favor is the kind of social grace that opens doors, gives access, and creates special opportunities. It can come from reputation, wealth, beauty, and biblically, even as a gift of God. Esther and Job found favor in the sight of the rulers of their day. Jesus grew in favor.

In the year of the favor of the Lord, no matter how much you had been disfavored, you could re-enter into God's favor. This release became a mighty expression of worship to God, a celebration of His very heart and nature to be extravagantly kind. His glory is demonstrated and manifested in the expression of this goodness and favor.

In claiming fulfillment of the year of the Lord's favor, Jesus was declaring His mission to liberate the physically, emotionally, spiritually, and relationally oppressed poor. His mission to us, the church, was to announce and demonstrate that those last on the world's list were going to be first on God's list of favor: that the disfavored were going to become the favored; that those considered wretched were going to be considered royalty; that the "left over" crowd was going to be at the front of the line in God's Kingdom.

I believe that as we bring worship and compassion to the poor, God wants us to help them not only with their physical needs, but also with a ministry that brings change and healing to their mindset: a healing of their self-esteem, and a restoration of the dignity of heart that comes from knowing they are created in the image of God. I have seen, over and over, that as we draw the poor through compassion into a life of intimate worship and fellowship with the Lord, He not only takes people out of poverty, He takes poverty out of people.

The wonderful thing about giving the gift of unmerited favor is that it reproduces itself in the life of the favored. The *gift* of favor can become a *weapon* of favor in the life of the recipient, which lifts them from poverty of heart, mind, or body. God is the only one who can bring ultimate healing. This healing includes the ability to be free from a "spirit of poverty," to be free and able to walk in a mindset of favor and sufficiency. This "favor mindset" breaks the power of poverty by releasing the poor to begin to operate in hope and faith.

Someone said that when you restore a person's ability to believe, you restore his or her ability to achieve. Hope for the future brings power in the present. Faith allows us to begin to see and appropriate resources in God that are not apparent to the natural eye.

I have seen the profound difference that comes into the life of people when through compassion, they see and are taught that they have been invited to live the rest of their lives in the Jubilee – the year of the favor of our God. They begin to move from a deficiency to a sufficiency mindset. As Jesus taught, "According to your faith, be it unto you" (Matt. 9:29, KJV).

One of the greatest examples I've ever heard of someone walking out of a poverty mindset and beginning to walk in a "favor mindset" was told by Wayne Myers, a missionary to Mexico, in his book *Living Beyond the Possible*. It is a story about Alberto.

> Near Matamoros, a village south of Mexico City, one church celebrated its anniversary for three days. They invited believers and unbelievers from the nearby villages, and a guest minister to speak at their evening services. It was a great opportunity to reach out to those who were not Christians, as everyone in Mexico – saint and sinner alike – loves a celebration.
>
> There was one problem. Hosting a celebration of that magnitude required food – lots of it. When they tallied up the cost of feeding everyone for three days, the church elders realized they would need a mir-

acle. How could a small village church feed so many people?

A woman stepped forward to supply all the chili peppers for the hot sauce. Another woman promised a three-day supply of beans. One man said he would provide the corn for the tortillas. Now all they lacked was the beef to make the tacos. But it was also the most expensive item on the list. No individual could afford three days' worth of meat to feed so many people. A silence fell over the group, killing the excitement and most of their faith. How were they going to find enough meat for the anniversary celebration?

"I'll bring the meat," said a brother from the back of the room. When they turned to see who had offered this generous gift, they were shocked that the voice belonged to Alberto, the poorest man in the church. He could hardly feed his own family and here he was offering to supply the most expensive item for the three-day meeting.

"Where are you going to get the meat?" the people wanted to know. "You don't even have a goat."

"I'll bring the meat," he said firmly.

Of course no one could rest until they knew how their poorest brother was planning to get the meat. They called another meeting and asked him when they could expect the meat, hoping he was going to explain his plan or back out of his promise.

"When do you need it?" he asked.

"The day after tomorrow," they replied. "We'll have to prepare our first breakfast at 6 AM and we will need the meat by then."

"All right, I'll have the meat to you by 6 AM but I will need six strong men and plenty of rope at my house by 4 AM tomorrow."

Six men volunteered, but they were still scratching their heads in bewilderment. Was the man not only poor but crazy, too? What if they started this meeting and humiliated themselves in front of the whole village?

On the morning of the first day of the meeting, six strong men with plenty of rope showed up at this Christian brother's house at 4 AM and found him waiting for them with an old battered rifle resting on his shoulder.

"Follow me," he said. "We're going hunting."

"And what will we hunt?" the men asked incredulously.

"Deer," he replied.

"We haven't had deer in this area for fifteen years," they scoffed.

Alberto started down the path. "Just follow me," he called over his shoulder. The men shrugged and set out with Brother Alberto, who began to praise God out loud for deer-meat tacos. They grumbled, but continued to follow close behind. At dawn, a buck jumped in front of them. Alberto, still praising God, said, "Lord, you aim the gun and I'll pull the trigger."

One bullet dropped the animal. Amazed, three of the men tied it with a rope to drag it home. Ahead, another buck, larger than his brother, stepped out on the path. After Alberto shot it, he turned around and calmly asked, "By the way, men, how many more do you want?"[1]

Wayne Myers goes on to explain:

Alberto knew what you and I sometimes forget – God owns all the cattle on a thousand hills. Everything we need is available through the currency of faith. If we are to be givers – people who are always looking for ways to invest in the Kingdom – we must also have faith in God's ability to supply what we don't have.[2]

The secret of favor is this. Those touched by kindness can become kind. Those who receive favor can believe God for even greater favor. In so doing, those who were the recipients become the change-agents for their neighbors. Truly, worship in combination with compassion not only rights wrongs and redresses physical lack, it imparts favor and destroys the spirit of poverty.

Giving Our Very Best to Those Who Have the Least

We have learned that one of the secrets to unleashing the favor of God through worship and compassion is giving our best, especially to those who have the least. Families are rarely excited about blessing and eating leftovers. In the same way, God is not as excited about blessing the gift of leftovers. Throughout scripture God always calls His people to give what is first, not what is left:

Honor the LORD with your possessions
And with the firstfruits of all your increase.
(Prov. 3:9, NKJV)

He wants the first of our time; the first of our money; the first of our service, energy, and creativity. God loves to bless excellence.

The Bible exhorts us in our worship to "make it glorious." We need to do the same whenever our worship includes compassion. Sadly, we often think of charity in terms of leftovers. The poor live within a second-hand economy. No wonder they often think of themselves as second-class citizens.

"To find the least among us and treat them like Jesus" has been called the highest expression of worship. At Heart for the World Church, we were so touched by this thought that we made it our motto: "Giving our very best to those who have the very least."

One person who has taught me much about excellence in compassion is Delane Bailey-Herd, project manager for Food for the Poor, Haiti, and founder of Hope Givers International. She has a special burden for the orphans in Zambia, and she loves to talk about "restoring the image and dignity of God among the poor." Her specialty is making little orphan boys and girls feel like princes and princesses. She teaches teams that excellence is not so much about *what* we give, but about the *kind of love* we show in giving – a love that honors, elevates, and esteems.

On her first trip to Zambia, Delane went along with a team in a supportive role. She had no official authority and really had few materials to give. One day as they came into a little African-bush village, Delane's heart was moved by the dozens of children looking on with curiosity about their visit. Suddenly a thought came to her mind. She had a towel, and she spotted a bucket of water that the local women had been using. Delane asked permission from the village chief to use the bucket and wash the children's hair. Everyone thought that was a strange idea, but the chief granted her permission.

These little boys and girls had seldom, if ever, had anyone wash their hair. Delane gently invited one little girl to go first. Delane sang and prayed over the little girl as she washed her hair, telling her how beautiful and precious she was. The little girl giggled with delight as she stood up to demonstrate the results of her beauty appointment. Well, that was it. Suddenly more kids than you could count lined up for their turn. For most of the day, Delane tirelessly gave honor to these children by washing their hair.

The chief was very impressed with Delane's kindness and invited her into his hut to speak with him and his wife. Quickly she discovered that he was very interested in, and open to, the gospel of Jesus Christ. Within a short time, he was bowing his head and receiving Jesus as the Lord and Savior of his life.

From that time on, we have made "beauty shop" a primary ingredient in our outreaches. Now we even include shampoo and barrettes as part of our ministry kits. This, of course, is not a new idea. Jesus first modeled this kind of worship and compassion when He washed the disciples' feet.

Here is a poem I wrote in March of 2002, after visiting the Philippines with a team, who along with the local churches, washed hair, made widows' hearts sing, and gave food to the hungry.

Faces of Mercy

How beautiful you seem, shining with shimmering
     light as on a diamond sparkling clean.
In dark and cruel places as an unexpected light,
Surprising sounds of love and laughter fill the air with
     praise in the darkness of night.
Sad faces illuminated with hope, break forth to say,
God is now among us, O what a happy day!

So gentle mercy comes, so simple are her deeds.
There is no fanfare, no great heroics tied to meeting
     needs.
Just great love, warmth, and kindness, sown like little
     seeds,
Given from the heart, those hungry little souls to
     feed.

Faces of mercy, you are so gentle, but O, your hands
     are strong.
For they work not just to comfort but to undo Satan's
     wrong.
Untiring they work and fight for justice and dignity to
     be restored,
They travail in spirit and body 'til God's holy image in
     a broken life is formed.

Don't be fooled by mercy's mild look and such,
For no stronger force in heaven or on earth exists than
     the power of Mercy's touch.
It is unstoppable, unquenchable, undefeatable, I say,
For though Hell fights against it, Mercy will win the
     day!

O sing, faces of mercy, so bright, so beautiful, so
     clear.
For whenever you sing, Heaven hushes to listen,
And the God of mercy draws near.

He rejoices over you and dances with you among
 those you dance beside.
He sings to the orphan, embraces the widow, and
 soothes the wounded's cries.
A swirl of glory and never-ending joy is waiting to be
 yours when eternity starts.
For you, faces of mercy have touched the Father's
 heart.

– Dale Walker

CHAPTER TWO – QUESTIONS

1. Think of some secular programs or attempts to bring relief to the poor and needy of the world. Observe the results of these programs. How do they differ from missions outreaches that bring the love of Jesus as a testimony in addition to needed physical provisions?

2. Have you ever participated in an activity or project that you didn't think you would like, and then found out that you actually had talent or proficiency in that task? How can you get involved in the regular operation of your church today?

3. Have you ever found yourself judging the needy? Have you ever given favor to someone you know didn't deserve favor? Try blessing an undeserving person in some way today, and see what God does with that.

4. Have you ever heard the old expression "Beggars can't be choosers?" Have you ever excused a lack of compassion with this attitude? When you hear God asking for tithes and offerings from your increase, do you "see" God in the lost and the poor, and envision giving your first-fruits to *them?*

CHAPTER THREE

WORSHIP AND COMPASSION AS A LIFESTYLE

Mercy Triumphs over Judgment

In the face of unkindness and injustice, compassion that has its focus on the Savior triumphs. James tells us to remember that "judgment without mercy will be shown to anyone who has not been merciful. Mercy triumphs over judgment!" (James 2:13, NIV). And Jesus himself instructed us to respond in this manner:

> *You have heard that it was said, "An eye for an eye and a tooth for a tooth." But I tell you not to resist an evil person. But whoever slaps you on your right cheek, turn the other to him also...love your enemies, bless those who curse you, do good to those who hate you,*

and pray for those who spitefully use you and persecute you.(Matt. 5:38-39, 44, NKJV)

However, the limits of compassion are beyond the feelings of natural man. We naturally feel hurt in the presence of unkindness. When we're faced with injustice, we so quickly feel indignation, rather than the compassion of Christ. Yet, we discover that miracles happen if our compassion is fed through worship, and we move beyond human judgment into mercy.

I love the words of the hymn "Rescue the Perishing" by Fanny J. Crosby that say:

> Down in the human heart, crushed by the tempter,
> Feelings lie buried that grace can restore;
> Touched by a loving heart, wakened by kindness,
> Chords that were broken will vibrate once more.

One of the ways we can live a lifestyle of worship and compassion is by choosing to stand where Jesus stood when faced with challenging situations. When we are criticized, talked about, let down, disappointed, or offended with another person's actions, the natural reaction is to feel "righteous" in the situation. We so easily stand in the position of judging who is right, who is wrong; who deserves kindness and respect, and who doesn't.

Jesus stood in this situation again and again – but each time He chose to feel and walk in compassion. The compassion of Jesus is so limitless. Why would he "feel" compassion for a thief who deserved to die and who was mocking and ridiculing Him. Why would He pray for those who hammered nails into His hands, "Father forgive them; for they know not what they do" (Luke 23:34, KJV). He was able to feel this way because He chose to feel the Father's heart of compassion. How do we step from the position of feeling righteous in a situation to feeling and walking in the compassion of Christ in a situation?

We take this step only by worshiping the Christ who chose to stand in compassion towards us personally: "while we were yet sinners, Christ died for us" (Rom. 5:8, KJV). In our suffering of wrong and injustice, we must remember Him:

> *"Who committed no sin, nor was deceit found in His mouth"; who, when He was reviled, did not revile in return; when He suffered, He did not threaten, but committed Himself to Him who judges righteously; who Himself bore our sins in His own body on the tree,...by whose stripes you were healed.* (1 Pet. 2:22-24, NKJV)

Peter says that if you choose to walk in His compassion towards the undeserving – "if you suffer for doing good and you endure it, this is commendable before God" (1 Pet. 2:20, NIV). This is worship and compassion at its *highest* level.

Actually, we sometimes more easily feel and show compassion for a physically poor person living in Africa than we do for a proud person living in our own home or neighborhood. This was the case with a neighbor my wife and I encountered, whom we called "Mr. Bob."

Mr. Bob was a gruff man in his early sixties when we first moved in across the street from him. He was a war veteran who wore a crew cut and had a major attitude towards life and people whose views differed from his own. He and his wife were well off financially, and they enjoyed traveling and participating in their various hobbies. Yet, in Bob's face, you could see a sadness and a loneliness caused by some deep regret in his life.

Mr. Bob had an immaculately trimmed yard of which he was very proud. One of the things that really irked him was when cats from the neighborhood would dig around and defile his beautiful garden. Finally, Mr. Bob couldn't take it anymore and resorted to purchasing cat traps. He would catch the cats in these traps and turn them over to animal control – a set up for a conflict, especially in my house. I happen to be married to a beautiful cat lover. My wife Sharon is such a kind and tolerant person, but when Mr. Bob caught her cat and sent "Frosty" to the slammer, that was more than her gentle heart could endure.

Because I don't share her fondness for cats, I found that I had plenty of grace to overlook this "little problem." My attitude didn't help Sharon one bit. Even though I was able to retrieve Frosty from animal control, for days Sharon struggled in her heart with this offense.

One day I was surprised to discover that she had made a plate of brownies for Mr. Bob. Sharon says the Lord spoke to her that "Mr. Bob doesn't need this plate of brownies, but you need to make them to help *you*." Through this simple act of obedience God did something special. She was clueless what to say when he came to the door. But as he opened the door our good and kind God gave her words of humility and repentance for Frosty's behavior. Mr. Bob was touched by this act of kindness, and Sharon's heart was set free. A short time later we noticed that the cat traps were gone. Far more important, a few years later we were able to pray the prayer of salvation with Mr. Bob, who had become a dear friend. We discovered again how Jesus can use our worship and compassion to reveal His love for the antagonists in our lives.

Small Things Done with Great Love

The greatest acts of worship through compassion are often the smallest unseen deeds – deeds hidden from men, but noticed by God. Jesus told us,

> *"So when you give to the needy, do not announce it with trumpets, as the hypocrites do in the synagogues and on the streets, to be honored by men. I tell you the truth, they have received their reward in full. But when you give to the needy, do not let your left hand know what your right is doing, so that your giving may be in secret. Then your Father,*

65

*who sees what is done in secret, will reward
you."* (Matt. 6:2-4, NIV)

I believe that Jesus taught that an act of compassion truly becomes an act of worship when it is done secretly for God's eyes, and not for the attention of men. He says that on Judgment Day, that which was "whispered in the ear in the inner rooms will be proclaimed from the roofs" (Luke 12:3, NIV).

I remember having the opportunity to go with my brother Tommy Walker and a team of world-class musicians on a concert ministry tour to the Philippines. I had the privilege of sharing the message at the worship evangelism concerts, which drew up to ten thousand people. The events were pretty spectacular, with lights, sounds, and stadiums. But I will always remember something that happened far away from the stage, far from the spotlights.

Our team visited a mercy maternity clinic where missionary midwives helped poor moms have healthy deliveries. Mercy in Action, led by Vicki Penwell, was an amazing ministry of compassion providing free delivery and prenatal care for desperately impoverished mothers. That ministry has brought life-saving care to thousands of moms and their babies in the Philippines and in other countries. The team at the maternity clinic was working hard under extremely difficult conditions.

On the day our group toured the clinic, we asked about their challenges and needs. They said that the most frustrating thing for the midwives was not a lack of medical supplies, not a rash of premature births, not inadequate funding, nor an overworked, understaffed team: it was the plumbing. It had not been working right for months, and they were having no luck at finding someone to fix it. You could see a look of desperation on their faces.

With no fanfare, a guy named Scottie – the band's bass player and an unbelievably gifted musician – said he understood plumbing and asked if he could help. So that day, while the rest of us were resting and preparing for a big concert that evening, Scott spent almost the entire day underneath the clinic's house, in the smothering Philippines heat, fighting the battle to bring victory to the plumbing. He ended up having just enough time to change his clothes and get to the concert that night.

At the end of our time there, the ladies from the clinic shared with tears of joy their thanks. They said the prayers we prayed were much appreciated, and that they had been blessed by the amazing worship concerts and events that we held. But without question, the act of worship that most touched their hearts – the act of selfless giving that would never be forgotten – was the gift of plumbing from Scott when he sacrificed his time and his agenda to fix a bunch of stopped-up pipes halfway around the world. Because of that gift, their ministry could go forward and the joy and morale of their entire team would remain high. Don't ever think less of your gift or the part God has given you to play than God does. Small, unseen acts of worship and compassion are always noticed by God, and often have the biggest impact on earth.

How to Throw a Kingdom Party

Jesus talked a lot about parties. On several occasions He taught that the Kingdom of God is like a party. He himself was criticized for being at parties with sinners. Of course, Jesus had some pretty interesting instructions for throwing parties. He taught that worship and compassion is intentionally inviting people to parties who cannot return the invitation:

> *"When you give a dinner or a supper, do not ask your friends, your brothers, your relatives, nor rich neighbors, lest they also invite you back, and you be repaid. But when you give a feast, invite the poor, the maimed, the lame, the blind. And you will be blessed, because they cannot repay you; for you shall be repaid at the resurrection of the just."*
> (Luke 14:12-14, NKJV)

The heart of God is that we delight in His presence and that we share His joy when we have Kingdom parties, especially with those most likely not to be invited to the parties of the world. It is as though Jesus wanted to announce through His ministry that those who would be last on the world's party list were sure to be first on His list. Once again, the Kingdom of God is all about giving the very best to those who have the very least.

Interestingly, I have found that it is the poor of this world, the physically and mentally challenged, who seem uniquely able to come into the joy of God's presence more easily and naturally than those whose lives are cluttered with the symbols of importance.

In 1999, I had the privilege of spending a few days in Hong Kong at one of the men's homes with St. Stephen's Society – a ministry established and directed by Jackie Pullinger. She tells the amazing story of God's transforming work among the most hardened and notorious heroin addicts in Hong Kong. The men in these homes have all come off the streets, and are for the most part, former hard-core heroin addicts. I had the joy of staying with a group of these recovering addicts. Never had I seen worship more passionate and real than with these lives that had been hopelessly bound but were now set free.

I was amazed just by being with them and seeing how Jesus had changed their lives. I learned so much from these men, and as the last night of my visit approached, I really wanted to bless them and thank them in a special way.

I decided the best way that I could bless them was to have a banquet in their honor. I asked the leader to describe their favorite kind of party, which turned out to be a barbecue: they loved barbequing chicken and beef over open charcoal fires. We went out and got all the meat that we could afford as the group set up their homemade barbeque grills over open fires. They made some really cool decorations for the party and set up a sound system for worship. When we returned, they started cooking. We were ready to go.

Suddenly, just about the time the party was to start, people began showing up from everywhere.

The yard started filling up with some of the scariest-looking people I had ever seen. Street sleepers, criminals, prostitutes, the homeless, and outcasts of every kind kept coming. What I didn't know was that while we were away buying meat, the guys went out into their streets and invited the most desperate people they could find to our party. I wish my response had been one of joy; however, it was anything but that. I was anxious and worried – about not having enough food, about fear of a police raid…

"What happened? Where did all of these people come from?" I asked the leader of the home.

"But Dale, you said you wanted to have a party," he replied. "Isn't this how Jesus said to throw a party? These are the people who would never invite us back."

I was convicted and humbled. "Brother, you are absolutely right. Let's party!"

And you know what? Jesus is delighted when the wretched are treated like royalty. I remembered the words Jesus spoke to John the Baptist as proof of His Messiah-ship. He said the Good News is being preached to "the wretched of the earth" (Matt. 11:5, MSG).

So many people turned out that there was just enough food for everyone to get a very small plate, but it really didn't matter. There was so much joy that night that the quantity of food took a back seat to the quality of worship and compassion. God's presence filled that yard: there was worship; there was prayer; there was laughter; and there was personal ministry to desperate people. Most importantly, Jesus came to that party. Again and again I saw the brothers praying over some desperate soul for salvation, deliverance, and healing. Moreover, as I saw prayers of salvation being prayed as the night went on, I had a whole new understanding of what makes a party a party: the thought of heaven rejoicing over one sinner being loved into the kingdom of God. I realized that true joy is not only *knowing* personally the ecstatic joy of being in God's presence, but also *sharing* the joy of God's presence with others. It is inviting and welcoming those who have never even once experienced God's parties.

One of the most powerful and exciting expressions of worship and compassion comes from learning how to throw a Kingdom party.

Friend of Sinners

As I have shared, one of the forms of worship and compassion that touches God's heart is being a friend of sinners and the poor. Jesus told us that anyone can greet and be kind to people who greet them and are kind to them in return. Common courtesy and protocol compel us to be friendly towards people like us, who are friendly towards us (Matt. 5:47). Our kindness becomes worship when it is given to the least deserving, to those who would more naturally be our enemies or our antagonists.

Jesus modeled this behavior, which offended the Pharisees: "Now the tax collectors and 'sinners' were all gathering around to hear him. But the Pharisees and the teachers of the law muttered, 'This man welcomes sinners and eats with them' " (Luke 15:1, NIV). However, Jesus continually brought the Father glory by welcoming sinners and by showing up in the homes of real stinkers like Zaccheaus. Jesus refused to be locked out of lives that were locked up in prisons of sin and corruption. After all, Jesus was not sent "into the world to condemn the world, but that the world through Him might be saved" (John 3:17, NKJV). His compassion towards Zacchaeus resulted in a radical response of worship. Zacchaeus actually ended up giving away half of his fortune to the poor, in a show of love for what Jesus had done in his life.

I met my own Zacchaeus when I was a nineteen-year-old Bible school student, and God really tested me on this point. He brought into my life a seventy-three-year-old man named Gordon. Gordon lived in the apartment across from me, and he was literally, figuratively, and every way imaginable, a "dirty old man."

Gordon was probably one of the vilest people I had ever met, and it seemed like the expressed mission in his later years was to lead me into temptation. The first time I met him he begged me to get drunk with him. He always wanted to talk to me, and tell me things I didn't want to hear. He told me it was obvious that my brother Steve, who was living with me at the time, was a holy man. But Gordon insinuated that both he and I *knew* that I was never cut out to be a Christian, and that my faith would soon fall apart.

Honestly, I wanted nothing to do with a man whom I thought to be a total reprobate. Still, my brother Steve encouraged me. He said that we should keep reaching out to Gordon in spite of himself. So we invited him to dinner and to watch football games with us. We prayed for him, forgave him, rebuked him – prayed some more – rebuked some more – and some more. We rebuked a lot. Yet somewhere in the process, and through this process, Gordon knew that we cared for him and loved him. He found every opportunity to be around us, and was even willing to go to church with us, because, as it turned out, we were the only friends he had left in the whole world.

I'll never forget one day when I was visiting him in his apartment, I could see that God had been wrestling with his heart. He had started reading the Bible and wanted to ask me questions. His main question was whether or not God could actually forgive someone like him – someone who had lived his entire life messed up. When we prayed, he literally fell on his knees and cried like a baby.

After the prayer, his first words to me were, "Dale, I promise, I swear, I will never sin again."

I laughed and told him, "That is a promise I am sure you can't keep. But even so, Jesus is going to be your Forgiver and Savior."

Not too long afterwards, Gordon made the last trip of his life – to El Paso, Texas, to attend my wedding. He brought a special wedding gift that he had spent almost three months making: a hand-stitched, needlepoint picture that says, "God Bless Our Home." Until then, I had no idea what a gifted artist Gordon

73

had been. That picture hangs in our kitchen to this day, more than thirty years later.

I saw Gordon one more time when he was literally on his death bed. We prayed, and I helped hold up his arms so he could worship. Gordon was such a special person. I will forever think of him as a "true stinker saved by grace," and I will hug him in heaven as one of my dearest friends.

CHAPTER THREE – QUESTIONS

1. Picture an undeserving person in your church, school, job or neighborhood. Try giving mercy to an undeserving person today. Do it on purpose even though your feelings are screaming "No!"

2. Can you think of a time when you helped someone with a mundane task, without thinking twice about it? Has a person ever come back later after you did that, and expressed gratitude for how much you had blessed them or changed their outlook on life?

3. Joyce Meyer said, "Salt doesn't salt salt!" Is there someone in your neighborhood or at your job who seems the least likely to fit into a church setting? Try inviting them to come to church with you, maybe even offering to give them a ride, if appropriate.

4. At church or at work, look over the crowd and mentally pick out two or three people whom you tend to avoid or perhaps even dislike for some reason, and write their names down on a list. Then *on purpose*, choose to greet one of them on a regular basis and get to know them better. When you begin to see that person as Jesus sees them, move on to the next person on your list.

CHAPTER FOUR

WORSHIP AND COMPASSION: THE CHILDREN

꽃

Caring for the Helpless Ones

One of the most profound ways that God uses worship and compassion is to help us confront the mystery of evil and suffering in our world, and in the lives it affects. Job is an example of millions of people today, who in the midst of their walk with God, encounter unexplainable suffering and pain.

We see in Job's story that God used worship, and later compassion, to help Job reconcile his sufferings with the goodness of God. He used worship and compassion to find a way to move beyond the evil, into the redemptive purposes God had for his suffering. The Bible makes it clear, "that God causes all things to work together for good to those who love God, to those who are called according to His purpose" (Rom. 8:28, NASB). Yet, when people are confronted with tragedy, it is very difficult for them to have peace and to believe in God's purposes.

Someone once described the events of our lives like pieces of a great quilt being sewn together by God as we move through this life. From our perspective we only see the backside of the design – the side which often looks chaotic and confusing. God, of course, sees the other side – the side of order and beauty, the side that shows the whole picture, just as He has designed it. He is creating it. He is working in it all things for our good, and He will show us that side some day.

The problem for us is to work through the dark emotions and deep emptiness that tragedies such as the death or injury of a loved one bring. Many people become poisoned by these events and aren't able to reconcile them with their relationship to a *loving* Father in heaven. But it is God's desire to use worship and compassion as part of the ministry of reconciliation – a ministry of restoring hope, peace, and meaning in the face of loss. He brings this ministry through us to others by compassion. The scripture says, "Rejoice with those who rejoice, and weep with those who weep" (Rom. 12:15, NKJV). The word *compassion* is derived from the Latin word that means "to suffer with."

Compassion calls us to go where it hurts; to enter into places of pain and brokenness. It requires us to feel weak with the weak, and vulnerable with the vulnerable. It means going to the places where people hurt, and being with them there. Compassion doesn't require us to explain the *why* of the suffering, but it does require us to move beyond our natural inclination to withdraw and to avoid the pain and difficulties of others, and simply be *present* with them in their suffering and their pain.

In the King James Version of the Bible, James 1:27 tells us that true religion is *being with* the orphans and the widows in their distress. Often, the gift God calls us to give the suffering is not an intellectual solution to their problem, but the gift of being with them – not a gift of *solving* but a gift of *being*. This is the gospel, not simply talked about, but demonstrated. It is the gospel of the Good Samaritan, who chose not to walk away, but to fully immerse himself in the suffering of another human being. It is the gospel of the incarnation. God, our Immanuel, chose to lay aside His divine prerogatives and fully become *with us,* immersed into our broken situation. I believe that "this gospel of the kingdom will be preached in the whole world as a testimony to all nations, and then the end will come" (Matt. 24:14, NIV).

Compassion helps suffering people find hope and faith again in the midst of their suffering. However, compassion by itself is not enough. To fully help a suffering person become reconciled with God in their situation, we must help lead people, through kindness and compassion, into *worship*.

When Job, through worship, laid His questions down at God's feet, the peace and presence of God came.

*I know that you can do all things, no plan of
yours can be thwarted. You asked, "Who is
this that obscures my counsel without knowledge?" Surely I spoke of things I did not
understand, things too wonderful for me to
know. You said, "Listen now and I will speak;
I will question you, and you shall answer me.
My ears had heard of you but now my eyes
can see you."* (Job 42:1-5, NIV)

As faith filled his heart, he could be sure of a
divine plan – a bigger destiny beyond the present
pain. Through that place of worship, he was actually able to find grace to pray for his unkind friends.
This undoubtedly helped drain some of the poison
out of his heart. Better still, Job was able to come
into a place of spiritual revelation about the infinite
wisdom and power of God. This fresh vision filled
his heart with faith and deepened his personal con-
tact and intimacy with God in a way that made him
say, "My ears had heard of you but now my eyes can
see you."

David seemed to have a similar experience
when he suffered the loss of the first son he had with
Bathsheba. He pleaded with God for his son's healing
and recovery. The Bible says that when David learned
of his son's death, he "got up from the ground. After
he had washed, put on lotions and changed his
clothes, he went into the house of the LORD and
worshiped" (2 Sam. 12:20, NIV). Something happened in the context of worship that brought healing,

79

reconciliation, and recovery into David's heart in his time of loss.

Job tells us, "The LORD gave and the LORD has taken away; Blessed be the name of the LORD" (Job 1:21, NKJV). Millions of people across the world have been blessed by Matt Redman's song "Blessed Be Your Name." The song speaks to this powerful dynamic: the act of offering worship, even when it is a sacrifice mixed with suffering. Those who learn this secret, find a calm and a compassion to move beyond themselves in their suffering. They are able to see their pain and their suffering used by God to bring hope and healing to others.

One of the most profound expressions of worship and compassion I have ever seen has been demonstrated by my brother Jerry and his wife Linda. Their son Jessie was born severely handicapped by cerebral palsy over twenty-nine years ago. Jessie can't walk, can't talk; he can't even turn over by himself. He is sustained by a feeding tube in his stomach. Jessie's circumstance is one of those mysteries that can't be solved in this life. Why did Jessie have to be born this way? Why hasn't he been healed, after countless prayers have been offered?

As is often the case, out of suffering, a depth of God's fellowship has emerged between parents and son that is truly amazing. Jerry and Linda will both say the greatest privilege of their lives is to be able to adore and serve Jesus in and through serving their son Jessie.

Jerry recently shared that,

Though Jessie is physically handicapped, there is definitely one area of his life where he is *not* handicapped. That is in his capacity to express uninhibited joy. Even in Jessie's brokenness he is filled with God's unstoppable life and joy. He laughs, even when we walk past his room. He roars with joy as he listens to his praise tapes. His greatest joy is just hanging out with us. There have been many days I was feeling so down when I've come home from work. But in the moments I spend caring for Jessie at the end of the day, something of his joy spills out on me, and I become liberated from my dark moods.

This is one part of a mystery – a kind of worship that might be described as "sharing with Christ in His sufferings": a form of worship that consists of laying your life down to serve someone who has suffered because of the brokenness of our fallen world. The other part of the mystery is that when you lay down your life, God allows you to take it up again in a way that is richer. As we empty ourselves on behalf of the suffering, God fills us fuller – fuller than had we even been seeking – and He sustains us so that we are able to stay full.

Jerry explains that,

As we wait with Jessie in his brokenness, we have also learned to keep our eyes completely fixed on Jesus Christ and his soon coming. We can already taste the victory, the vindication of justice, the triumph that Jessie will own the moment Christ appears. The ultimate crescendo of worship we are waiting for will be experienced in that moment when bodies are changed; wheel chairs are pushed away; the beds of the bedridden are deserted forever; the dance of those who've never walked begins; the song of those who've never sung bursts forth; and we who have shared in their suffering get to be the first to share in their explosive dance of victory. Come quickly Lord Jesus!

Let the Little Children Come

There is no way to discuss worship and compassion without talking about Christ's invitation to experience His presence by holding and receiving a little child. Jesus said, "Whoever humbles himself as this little child is the greatest in the kingdom of heaven. Whoever receives one little child like this in My name receives Me" (Matt. 18:4-5, NKJV).

I can testify how true this really is. I remember one spring day the phone ringing and the shocked look on my wife's face when the voice on the other end of the line asked without warning, "Do you want my baby?"

The details gradually came forward: a baby girl had been born to this severely drug- addicted mother, and the baby herself was going through life-threatening withdrawals, fighting for her life in the infant ICU of the county hospital. The social workers had already told the mother that there was no way they were going to allow her to keep the baby.

Sharon and I already had five children, and our youngest had just started kindergarten.

We were convinced we were starting a new season of life. Isn't it funny how some of God's biggest blessings in our lives start off with what seems to be jolting interruptions to our plans?

We drove down to the hospital to meet baby "Hope" (that was the birth name her biological mother had given her).

What we saw just broke our hearts: this tiny little infant, with tubes and wires attached to every imaginable part of her body, curled up in a little ball, screaming her heart out with pain.

The doctors said they really couldn't give us a prognosis. They simply had no idea what her future recovery would be like.

We left the hospital unsure, with just a few hours to make a life-altering decision. When we arrived home, the March NCAA basketball tournament was on the TV. Just as we were walking into the room a public service announcement came on. The commercial began with a picture looking into an ICU ward. Over the top of the door, in huge letters, were the words *Born Losers.*

As the doors opened, the camera focused in on "crack babies" going through withdrawals, each one reminding us of the little baby we had just seen. The message went on to tell of the horrible effects drugs have on a child when the mother is a user during pregnancy. It explained that many of these babies are destined for lives of failure and despair.

At that moment, Sharon felt the Holy Spirit speak to her heart, saying, "I'm going to show you what I can do with born losers."

Nineteen years later, our daughter Molly is a bright, beautiful young lady, who attends the university and has a dream of becoming a nurse-midwife, and of helping suffering children here and on the mission field. As a camp counselor to younger girls, she has already preached the Good News. That little girl with the special gift of knowing how to touch her Daddy's heart has come a long way. For us, her presence became a confirmation of our calling and our passion: To help turn those whose lives seem hopeless into those whose lives are victorious, with an unstoppable hope and future through Jesus Christ.

We didn't think of it at the time, but when we received that hurting child into our home, Jesus brought His presence into our lives in a way greater than we could have ever imagined.

To Save a Remnant

I remember in a time of personal devotion just asking the Lord this question: "Where are the next Billy Grahams, D. L. Moodys, Josephs, Esthers, and Davids?" I sensed strongly that the answer was, "One of them just died of starvation in Sudan. Another was sold into child prostitution in Thailand. Oh, she was born with AIDS in South Africa..."

From the beginning of time, Satan's chief target has always been the children. The demonic evil of child warfare has had many ugly manifestations through rulers and leaders such as Herod, Pharaoh, and Hitler. However, behind all the forms of evil attacks devised against children is the original murderer, Satan himself. In chapter 12 of the book of Revelation, it is written: a "sign appeared in heaven – a great, fiery red dragon having seven heads and ten horns." The scripture says that "the dragon stood before the woman who was ready to give birth, to devour her Child as soon as it was born" (verses 3-4, NKJV).

I think of this child as not only picturing Jesus, but also the holy remnant of God's chosen throughout history – especially the little children he has destined to advance His Kingdom in their generation. Without question, the love and praises of the little children touch the Father's heart in a special way – and they are especially significant weapons of spiritual warfare against spiritual darkness.

As Jesus enjoyed the children shouting in the temple area after His triumphal entry, "Hosanna to the Son of David" (Matt. 21:15, NIV), He spoke to the religious elite present who were indignant about the kids praising him. He quoted Psalm 8 and said,

Have you never read,
"Out of the mouth of babes and nursing infants
You have perfected praise"? (Matt. 21:16, NKJV)

Psalm 8 clarifies what perfected praise does:

Out of the mouth of babes and nursing infants
You have ordained strength,
Because of Your enemies,
That You may silence the enemy and the avenger. (verse 2, NKJV)

It is no wonder that Satan wants to destroy the holy seed, and that the heart of all spiritual warfare today is a fight for the children. According to statistics from 2002, six million children under the age of five die each year as a result of hunger.[1] According to World Vision's website, more than twenty-four thousand children under the age of five die daily of preventable causes.[2] Again, the enemy knows that whoever wins the children, wins the future of nations.

Over the last thirteen years, our focus through Heart for the World Ministries has been to help local churches in developing nations – those operating on the front lines of poverty – reach out to rescue and restore malnourished children. One of my greatest joys has been seeing these children not only restored, but raised up in faith, to begin to be transformers of their families and their communities.

This is part of the promise of Isaiah 58. The Lord said as we share our bread with the hungry and lift injustice, we will raise up the foundations of many generations… (these that are touched) will be called the Repairers of the Breach (intercessors) who will also become the Restorer of Streets (building new avenues of Hope) for others to dwell in.

One of these restorer/transformers is Mark John – a graduate of a feeding program in a *barangy* (neighborhood) called Sitros Veterans on the outskirts of Manila, Philippines. He is now thirteen years old, and he came to Christ, along with his brother, because of the Hope Center feeding ministry of the Living Body of Christ, led by Pastor Steve Mirpuri. Not only was

Mark John saved from malnutrition as a young child, but he also developed a deep passion for his family to be saved. His dad was a hardened drunkard and a very violent man; his mother, very sad and abused.

However, Mark John was not intimidated by his family's circumstances. Instead, he began praying for their salvation. Sure enough, one day, his mother came to the center and gave her life to Jesus. His dad was a different story. Though Mark John would beg his dad to receive Jesus, he would simply push his son away. For over a year, Mark John and his mother kept praying every day for his dad's salvation.

One day, while working as a security guard, his dad encountered a robber and was shot in the ensuing conflict. His dad was rushed to the hospital, and because of the seriousness of the injury, everyone – including Mark John's dad – thought he was going to die. But Mark John was praying. Somehow on the ride to the hospital, this dad regained consciousness long enough to realize what was going on. He cried out to God in prayer for salvation, and a miracle of healing began to occur. In fact, he was out of the hospital in a very short time, miraculously healed on the outside and a completely changed man on the inside.

Mark John's father became an elder in his church, and he gave his testimony in an outdoor evangelistic rally where I spoke several years ago. I have never seen a family more united and on fire for Jesus than this family. Truly, the prayers and praises of a child silenced the avenger and brought perfected praise to the throne of God.

Worship and compassion for children leads to restoration of families, communities, and sometimes, even nations: "They will rebuild the ancient ruins and restore the places long devastated; they will renew the ruined cities that have been devastated for generations" (Isa. 61:4, NIV).

CHAPTER FOUR – QUESTIONS

1. How difficult is it for you to not give advice to people who obviously need it (in your opinion)? Did you ever go into someone's house and mentally rearrange their furniture and repaint their walls (or worse, mentally wash their dishes or mop their floors)? Have you ever avoided people who suffered a tragedy in their life, because you felt you couldn't help them "fix it," or didn't know what to say?

2. Play a game with yourself or your family by pretending to be mute and not able to speak, perhaps at the dinner table. You are only allowed to use gestures and hugs to relay *positive* feedback, otherwise remain silent. Did you learn something that you never noticed or realized before? Did the others appear to enjoy your silent presence? Now you can take what you learn into the neighborhood and just be there for someone whose circumstances seem hopeless. Make sure to pray for peace and strength for that person on a regular basis.

3. Can you spot some born-losers in your life experiences? Can you picture God giving up on them? Perhaps you were a born-loser with a testimony of a divine re-birth that you can share with others to encourage them.

4. Children tend to have heaps more faith than adults. Next time you have an ache or pain, or something worse, try going to your children, or to a Sunday school class, and ask them to pray for you. Do it in faith believing, then stand back and watch what happens. Your faith, as well as theirs, will be bolstered, and will reinforce the awareness that we need to make prayer a priority in our lives.

CHAPTER FIVE

GLOBAL COMPASSION

Worship outside the Box

When God wants to do a greater work *through* our lives, He first gives us a greater vision *for* our lives. Before God can maximize our ministry to Him and to others, He first maximizes our vision and our dreams.

Someone said, "The size of our nets determines the size of our catch." I've also heard someone say that our visions generally come in one of four sizes:

- a cap-size vision – a vision for myself
- an umbrella-size vision – a vision for me and my spouse
- a car-size vision – a vision for my family
- a church-size vision – the size of my church

However, more sizes exist. For instance, some people can grasp a stadium-size vision – a vision for their community. But I believe the vision God wants us all to see is for the whole world. Today, God is urging us to expand our vision in the same way he instructed the Israelites in the book of Isaiah:

Enlarge the place of your tent, stretch your tent curtains wide, do not hold back; lengthen your cords, strengthen your stakes. For you will spread out to the right and to the left; your descendants will dispossess nations and settle in their desolate cities. (Isa. 54:2-3, NIV)

God is also showing us something similar to what He showed Abraham in Genesis 15:5. He is inviting us to "come outside" of our tent (the box of our present thinking), and look at the stars of the heavens: "so shall your descendants be" (NKJV).

A few years ago fast-food restaurants came up with the concept of *supersizing* our meals. In a similar way, God wants to *globalize* our vision for what he can do through us and through our church ministry. Too often we have thought of worship and compassion within the limited scope of our church building or our congregations. However, I like to think of worship as a glorious diamond too beautiful to just leave in a box. It needs to be displayed. When the world sees authentic worship, especially along-side of compassion, they will be drawn to Christ, and communities will be changed.

I love the story of Paul and Silas in the Philippian jail (Acts 16:25-34). They refused to let their worship be confined. At midnight – right there in the jail cell among all the other prisoners – they sang and worshiped God. God joined their choruses, breaking chains and opening prison doors with an earthquake. Their worship was followed by a powerful act of compassion towards the jailer. They chose not to escape, but to stay and save the life and the soul of the jailer, and eventually, the souls of his family. What a testimony of the power of expanding worship and compassion.

To be in harmony with God's worship vision, we must think of far more than a congregation of worship. We need to think in terms of seeing the nations worship and bow down.

Psalm 67 is a powerful psalm of global worship. The Psalmist writes:

> *May God be gracious to us and bless us*
> *and make his face shine upon us,*
> *Selah*
> *that your ways may be known on earth,*
> *your salvation among all nations.*
> *May the peoples praise you, O God;*
> *may all the peoples praise you.*
> *May the nations be glad and sing for joy,*
> *for you rule the peoples justly*
> *and guide the nations of the earth.*
> *Selah*
> *May the peoples praise you, O God;*
> *may all the peoples praise you.*
> *Then the land will yield its harvest,*
> *and God, our God, will bless us.*

God will bless us,
and all the ends of the earth will fear him.
(NIV)

God introduced me to a call of global worship and compassion in a surprising way when I was busy pastoring a church in El Paso, Texas. I liked the thought of missions, but concluded I was way too busy just trying to keep up with what I thought were the overwhelming needs of our little congregation and community. A missionary friend called and asked if I would like to have a pastor from the Philippines share a testimony at our Sunday night service. Ordinarily, I would have said, "No." But for some reason, I felt compelled to say, "Yes, have him come."

Brother Levi Ramoyong shared with our church his testimony of being called to lead a church-planting movement among the poor and destitute people in the Philippines. As he spoke, something began melting in my heart, and tears welled up. After I accepted an invitation to come visit his work, the burden for the poor and for missions continued to build in me. One night I felt captured by a sense of calling from the Holy Spirit to minister among the people I had met in the Philippines.

Sometime later, I told my wife that I felt we were supposed to move to the Philippines as missionaries. She didn't feel the same conviction, and really felt that we should pray more about that. As we did, it became clear that God wasn't calling us to *leave* our church, but that He was calling us to *take* our church to the Philippines, and to the nations. Through prayer with our elders, we concluded that God's plan was for us to *tithe* a portion of our church finances and efforts, and for me to *tithe* a portion of my time, toward leading our church in ministry to the nations.

I distinctly remember the first time announcing that I would be going for a month to pray and minister in the Philippines. Many expressed concerns, and some even suggested that the church was going to fall apart because of this decision. I did go, and a most amazing thing happened. Not only did God use us in the Philippines, but our church grew by over two hundred members in the following couple of months. I have often joked that the real secret to church growth is for the pastor to leave!

Actually what we saw was the fulfillment of a word I felt the Lord was giving us: that if we would seek to flow with His heart for the nations, He would care for us and bless us beyond what we could have envisioned. Later I discovered that this is really the heart of the Abrahamic promise, and what is expressed in Psalm 67.

God's purpose is to bless us – to allow His face to shine upon us so that the nations of the earth might be blessed. God has promised to bless those whose aim is to be a blessing. We made a twenty-four-year commitment to the Philippines to give at least one month of ministry each year. We are now in year twenty, and I can testify that God has blessed us in every way, beyond our imagination, as we have followed His leading, and His heart for the nations.

Faith That Works Through Love

There's something about going and holding a child.

On one of my trips to the Philippines, I had a life-changing experience in a graveyard. I was invited by a mission ministry to minister to people who lived in a cemetery in the middle of Cebu City, the second largest city in the Philippines. While there, I discovered that many of the poorest of the poor are squatters – unable to afford to buy or rent any place to live. Instead, they set up shacks of cardboard or other discarded materials on whatever vacant spots they can find.

In Cebu City, there were literally hundreds of people who had decided the best place for them to live was among the graves of a cemetery. The graves there are often built as above-ground cement vaults. These people would actually use the cement structures for tables and beds, and as part of their living quarters.

That day, I went to share worship and compassion with the people, taking along a guitar and some snacks. We were, of course, swarmed by excited children as we came into the cemetery. But I will never forget one little girl, not more than three years old, just skin and bones really, wearing a tattered shirt for a dress. She came running up to me, holding up her arms, wanting me to pick her up. I swung my guitar over my shoulder and lifted her up. I prayed a little prayer over her and tried to put her down. She would have none of it. Instead, she just dug her fingers into the back of my neck as if to say, "Please don't put me down, I want you to hold me." After a couple more attempts to put her down, each with the same result, I decided that she would be mine to carry for the rest of the outreach. I actually went on to play the guitar with this little girl around my neck and to preach a message with her still holding on.

At the end of the outreach, I was overwhelmed with a sense of God's presence. I heard the Lord telling me, "Look at her, Dale. You have four daughters, what would you do if one of them were living in these conditions?"

"Lord, I would do anything to care for them – no price would be too great."

"They are *all* my daughters," the Lord said. "I did not bring you seven thousand miles to preach a sermon. I brought you seven thousand-plus miles from the other side of the world to hold one child who doesn't have a father in her life. And I wanted to use your hands and your heart to express my Father's heart of love for her. Do you realize that their greatest need is just to know my Father's heart? I tell you, I am waiting to open the windows of Heaven and pour out resources upon those willing to be channels of my mercy to children like this one."

When despair had a face and a name and eyes, I understood poverty.

Later, I sensed the Lord saying that He wanted to pour out a "Joseph anointing." Joseph was, of course, a man with no means in himself. He was a prisoner, in fact. But God gave him a vision and a dream, and he went on to feed the nations, and save them from starvation. I took that day as an invitation to ask God to open the resources of Heaven and to allow our church and our partners to feed the nations, beginning in the Philippines. I remember being led to ask, not just for truckloads, but for *shiploads* of food for hungry children. I committed to helping the missionaries in that location start a feeding program for these children. I made that commitment, even though I did not have the money, and didn't know where the money would come from.

The next day, we left the Philippines and headed to Nagoya, Japan, where we had been invited to minister in a church that Sunday. I shared about my experience in the graveyard, and I will never forget what I witnessed that day. God poured out a "spirit of generosity" upon this precious Japanese congregation of believers. People cheerfully emptied their wallets; some even went home to get additional money.

As we were leaving for the airport that afternoon, cars literally followed us to the airport. People came running after us to give offerings for the children in the Philippines. By the end of the day, over forty thousand dollars had been given – enough to feed the children in that community and over one thousand more children in other communities for a whole year. That was 1999. Today, Heart for the World Ministries continues to provide food for over three thousand children not only in the Philippines, but also in Mexico, Honduras, Zambia, Thailand, and among the poor in the U.S.

Through all of this, I learned something wonderful about faith. Faith works through love. And what really matters, as Paul noted in Galatians 5:6, is "faith working through love" (NKJV).

When we allow God to move extravagantly in our heart with compassion, we can find ourselves filled with faith to move mountains on behalf of hurting and suffering people. When God gives you a great love for people, he doesn't leave you helpless to respond to the needs you see. When God gives you compassion, He also pours out faith, to ask and believe for miracles.

I have been impressed in studying the miracles of Jesus' ministry, just how often miracles of faith are associated with expressions of Christ's heart of compassion for people. For example in Matthew 9:35-36, it is written,

> *Jesus went about all the cities and villages, teaching in their synagogues, preaching the gospel of the kingdom, and healing every sickness and every disease among the people. But when He saw the multitudes, He was moved with compassion for them, because they were weary and scattered, like sheep having no shepherd.* (NKJV)

I believe here we see a model, *the* model really: great faith starts with great love and compassion. As we have been learning, worship is not just about blessing God's heart; it is about allowing God to break our hearts for the poor and hurting. As He breaks our heart, He puts in our hands the keys to the storehouses of heaven. He urges us to dream big, and to ask big. He wants us to attempt great things for His glory among the lost, the least, and the poor.

The Riches of Compassion Flowing Out of the Recognition of Our Poverty

Who are the poor?

That's a question I have found myself asking after visiting many places around the world, and spending time with those who have the least of this world's goods. In James 2:1-5, the writer warns us to be very careful about treating the rich with favoritism. He cautions us against the mistake of imagining that those with financial wealth are those most likely to add value to our fellowship and spiritual lives. He says, "Listen, my beloved brethren: Has God not chosen the poor of this world to be rich in faith and heirs of the kingdom which He promised to those who love Him?" (verse 5, NKJV).

In America, one of the worst kinds of poverty we have is the poverty of materialism. It blinds us to our own spiritual poverty, and makes us unable to receive the *true riches* of spiritual wholeness and contentment that come from a life of simple faith. As I have fellowshipped with believers who subsist with very little of this world's wealth, I have been shocked and stunned by their *joy,* which in turn exposes the lack of trust and contentment in my heart. I have cried as I have visited pastors in the third world whose homes were no more than straw huts; yet, I have seen them and their children worshiping God and laughing for joy, with just a bowl of rice and bits of fish to eat – insisting that I sleep on the one bed that they have.

In the first century, the church at Laodicea exemplified a state of material prosperity and, at the same time, was spiritually poor. In Revelation, Jesus urges them to discover their true state of spiritual poverty, and not to hide it behind what they can buy, or behind what image of importance their wealth can give them in the eyes of others. He is begging them not to shrivel up into an emaciated state of spiritual "skin and bones." He said if they would acknowledge their weakness and poverty before the Lord, He would give them fresh revelation of His presence among them, so they could fellowship with Him in worship in a deeper, more intimate way. Moreover, He would clothe and cover their nakedness with white linen:

Because you say, "I am rich, have become wealthy, and have need of nothing" – and do not know that you are wretched, miserable, poor, blind, and naked – I counsel you to buy from Me gold refined in the fire, that you may be rich; and white garments, that you may be clothed, that the shame of your nakedness may not be revealed; and anoint your eyes with eye salve, that you may see. (Rev. 3:17-18, NKJV)

We know from Revelation 19:8, that these garments of fine linen are "the righteous acts of the saints." They are works of love and compassion that will be greatly rewarded. If we stay in a broken place before God, He will produce works through us that will be rewarded in the end. We won't have to stand on Judgment Day with burned-up wood, hay, and stubble.

One of the lessons I have re-learned lately is that a life of worship and compassion has to be continuously renewed. I even talk about that in the first chapter (in the section titled "Worship – The Oil of Compassion"). However, I am truly amazed at just how easily our love becomes lukewarm, how quickly our vision becomes darkened by self-interest.

For instance, even during the writing of this book, I had an experience in which I did not act compassionately because I needed renewal. A couple traveling through town came in during the middle of a meeting I was having with some of the leaders of our church. The travelers were tired, hungry, and in need, and had nowhere to go, but I was in a meeting, and I was irritated that they were interrupting us. I purposely ignored them until my wife Sharon got up and went to help take care of their needs.

Later she kindly rebuked me. "What happened?" she asked. "I can't remember a time you didn't run to help someone who was hungry and in need."

I ducked her rebuke at the time, but later I stood convicted before the Lord. I cried out, "Dear Lord, here I am writing a book on worship and compassion, and I am the guy who lost my compassion. I desperately need You to come and heal my lukewarm-ness and renew my passion for You and compassion for people." I honestly believe that God answered that prayer. I was reminded again that the only way to stay fresh before the Lord in compassion and worship is to stay broken before the Lord in admitting and surrendering my weakness before Him.

I love what Jim Cymbala, pastor of The Brooklyn Tabernacle, shared about weakness in his book *Fresh Wind, Fresh Fire*. He said, "I discovered an astonishing truth: God is attracted to weakness. He can't resist those who humbly and honestly admit how desperately they need Him."[1]

The only way we will ever stay strong in worship and compassion is to stay weak and desperate before God. Jesus said, "Blessed are the poor in spirit, For theirs is the kingdom of heaven" (Matt. 5:3, NKJV). We cannot truly touch and bless the heart of God, or the lives of the poor and the broken, unless we can learn to stay continually aware of our poverty before the Lord.

A Strategy for Worship and Compassion

I want to close with some practical suggestions on how to grow in a lifestyle and ministry of worship and compassion.

First, I want to encourage local churches to dare to believe that God has called them to be on the front lines in response to the need for global compassion. Though we should all be very grateful for the work of international relief and development agencies, we should not expect them to carry all of the responsibility *for us*. They cannot do the work alone.

Although the AIDS epidemic appears to be spreading faster than any of the organizations being formed to deal with the crisis, I believe there is one organization that is growing as fast, or in fact faster, than the crisis – and that is the church of Jesus Christ.

We have the opportunity to do what government agencies and even billionaire philanthropists *cannot do*: share the love of Christ. We have the opportunity to see millions of ordinary believers, in hundreds of thousands of ordinary local churches, mobilized into armies of worship and compassion – armies that can change the world in extraordinary ways before Jesus comes back.

At a time when natural disasters and catastrophes seem to be growing, massive epidemics are multiplying, and the number of people starving and dying (especially among the children) is skyrocketing in developing nations, the need for a new emphasis on worship and compassion is crucial and paramount. Many churches are beginning to step up to this call. Churches like Saddleback Church have taken the lead with ministries like the PEACE initiative, a worldwide ministry. PEACE stands for Promote reconciliation, Equip servant leaders, Assist the poor, Care for the sick, and Educate the next generation. Other churches, like the Antioch Church from Waco, Texas, provided the very first wave of relief and rescue workers to reach the tsunami victims in Southern Asia, just a few short days after the tsunami hit at the end of 2004. We have also seen, in an amazing way, the unprecedented leadership of churches in response to the Hurricane Katrina disaster in 2005.

In the midst of the world's pain and suffering, the hope and power of the gospel is most obviously displayed. Every local church can have a significant impact in this regard, both locally and globally.

This leads me to the second suggestion: I believe an effective strategy to build, equip, and deploy armies of worship and compassion is to start to give *locally,* even as we are all learning to think globally. We should go to our neighborhood with an eye to the nations.

Our church's decision to get involved began with a commitment to share whatever we had with our neighbors, and *then* to share with the nations. We identified a public elementary school attended by children of some very poor families and developed a program to give groceries – through the school – to families in need. At the same time, we started helping local churches, working on the front lines of poverty in developing nations, to provide feeding programs for malnourished children. In the same way, we have offered medical supplies and educational materials to churches in developing nations to distribute. We have found that, on a weekly basis, we can send teams to do worship and compassion ministry in the *neighborhood* – and on a monthly basis we can send teams to the *nations*. Admittedly, the nations are readily accessible to our church because we live on the border with Mexico. But the location of your church should not dictate the focus of your vision for worship and compassion.

We encourage everyone to make it a priority to practice worship and compassion locally *and* globally. We have found that simple activities like those described earlier – such as food giveaways, parties for the poor, visits to nursing homes and prisons, and outreach lunches for the homeless – bring amazing results in both the givers and the receivers.

We have also found that *partnership* is the third key to making a global impact. Heart for the World Ministries is a separate, nonprofit organization that was formed to work as a partnership of churches, businesses, ministries, and individuals who share a common vision. Our vision is to give hope and a future through Jesus Christ to the poorest of the poor around the world; to accomplish something together that none of us can accomplish alone; and to mobilize armies and resources of worship and compassion for God's redemptive causes in the earth.

In the last year, we have organized mission trips and relief offerings from over fifty other churches, including churches in Japan and other nations of the world. God loves unity. He supremely blesses efforts to do together what none of us could do alone for the poor of the world. Mother Teresa said, "What I can do, you cannot. What you can do, I cannot. But together we can do something beautiful for God."[2]

Finally, I want to encourage each of you individually. What an amazing difference you can make! There is a fire inside of you that can spread across the earth. Yet it is so easy to become overwhelmed by the need. It is easy to feel like, "What's the use? Whatever I have to give or bring is just a drop in the ocean. Where would I even start?"

That's why I love God's word to Moses in Exodus 4:1-3. Moses said,

> *What if they do not believe me or listen to me and say, "The LORD did not appear to you"? Then the LORD said to him, "What is that in your hand?" "A staff," he replied. The LORD said, "Throw it on the ground."* (NIV)

The Lord said to just put down whatever you have in your hand. It doesn't have to be much. It doesn't have to be big. In fact, it isn't really about *what* you give. It is all about what an infinite, all-powerful God *can do* with what you give. He is the God who can take five little loaves and fishes and feed five thousand men, besides the women and children. He can take a spark of love and compassion and set a forest ablaze.

Leadership author John Maxwell frequently says that one is too insignificant a number to achieve anything great. And he's right. But sometimes, an entire move of God begins with one: one person, one small gift, one single act of obedience, one demonstration of worship and compassion. That is why one of the greatest heroes of my life has been my nephew, Charlie.

Charlie was born to my sister and brother-in-law, Janey and Sam Stewart, who for many years were missionaries in Guatemala City, Guatemala. Charlie was born with a serious heart defect and had to have several critical heart surgeries just to survive. As he grew up, there was something extremely special about Charlie. He loved Jesus, and he loved to give, especially to other children.

On his very first day of kindergarten, Charlie was excited about eating the lunch his mother Janey had packed for him. At lunch time, Janey went to the school to see how Charlie was doing. She was surprised to discover a classmate named Micah eating Charlie's lunch. When she asked her son about this, Charlie simply explained that Micah was hungry. So he joyfully gave his lunch to Micah.

Charlie extended this simple act of kindness and generosity to other kids in Guatemala over and over. If he had a pack of Life Savers, you could be sure he was going to find someone to share them with. When he went with his dad to minister to the poor, Charlie always returned home with less than he started with, giving whatever he could to a needy child. Shortly before Charlie was thirteen years old, his heart finally gave out, and Charlie went home to be with the Lord. It was an unspeakably painful loss, especially for Charlie's mom and dad.

A year or so later, while Janey was still dealing with the overwhelming grief, and praying for God to help her find a way through it, she heard a knock at the door. There stood four little street kids asking for something to eat. Just then, the thought came to Janey, "I can give them what would have been Charlie's lunch!" The boys took the lunch, and the next day there were eight kids at her door. That was the beginning of a new ministry that has become known across the world as Charlie's Lunch – a ministry headquartered in El Paso, Texas, and led by Sam and Janey Stewart, Charlie's parents. This ministry serves meals through local churches in developing countries around the world. Recently, they celebrated the serving of the one-millionth lunch. It all started with the compassion of a kindergarten boy, and the gift of one meal to a hungry classmate.

God is waiting to multiply the miracle of compassion through whatever you have in your hand. It may be time; it may be prayer. It may be a warm meal, a simple visit, a letter, or a phone call. Maybe the lives you are going to change are not in a country across the world. Maybe they are in the other room in your own home.

The place to start is worship. Begin to respond in gratitude to God for all that He has done for you in Christ. Then, expect Christ to fill your heart with a thought, an idea, or a way to simply touch a person's life. As you extend your worship into compassion, you too will become part of the revolution that is changing the world through love.

CHAPTER FIVE – QUESTIONS

1. Walking in compassion means overcoming the forces of indifference (cynicism, fear, ignorance, isolation). When was the last time your heart broke and was burdened for a co-worker or a neighbor to find Christ in his or her life?

2. How big is your vision of your role in God's kingdom? Your church's role? Do you need to pray for more compassion? What areas of comfort in your life would you be willing to give up for more service time in the Kingdom?

3. Do you ever turn off the TV or change the channel when those charity programs come on showing the little starving kids in Africa, India, or South America? What would happen if you made yourself watch next time? Have you ever been led to send them money, maybe even felt drawn to going to one of those places? Or maybe you felt it would be a hopeless drop in the bucket. Is there perhaps a child like one of them on your back doorstep whom you never see?

4. In what ways do you notice that you seem to be losing steam, or settling down into a comfort zone of idleness? What can you do to rekindle your "first love"?

5. What are some short-term outreaches currently available at your church in which you can participate? Have you participated in them before? How did God bless you during and after giving of yourself to His needy?

ADDITIONAL QUESTIONS

1. Can you think of one person who might be crying, "No one cares for my soul"?

2. Ask yourself, "Am I unresponsive to the hurting?" If so, ask yourself why.

3. Where would Jesus go if He came to your hometown?

4. Whom do we see as our neighbor? When we see the wounded in our everyday lives, do we ask, "How can I help?"

5. Has there been a time during worship when you felt *completely* ministered to, and then you were empowered to minister to another? Describe what happened.

6. This week, try praying: "Lord, do something in my heart that will cause others to be drawn to and touched by Jesus." Report back on your experience.

7. Apart from God, what person, place, or thing in your memory most represents kindness? Why?

8. What do you find is the easiest excuse to use for not being kind to someone else?

    A. I'm too busy.
    B. I've had a hard day.
    C. They are always asking for things.
    D. They're not kind to me.
    E. I've got to take care of my own needs first.

F. If I'm kind, they might expect more from me than I'm able to give.

9. Where do you most need God's kindness to fill you? It's sometimes hard for me to be kind because

    A. I'm exhausted physically, emotionally, and spiritually. I feel like I have nothing more to give.
    B. I've been dumped on and treated unfairly. I have anger blocking out any compassion that might have otherwise been there.
    C. I'm disappointed and discouraged with life and can't seem to get my mind off of my own problems enough to really be kind.
    D. I feel worthless and like a failure with nothing to give to anybody.

10. Describe an example of what it feels like to receive undeserved favor.

11. "God, open the floodgates of mercy in my heart towards _____" (fill in a name).

12. When it comes to compassion, what best describes the condition of your heart?
A. Eager B. Hardened C. Tired D. Suspicious

13. Describe an area of ministry that you feel the river of mercy carrying you to.

JOURNALING EXERCISES

A. Compassion

The following statements describe ways we can think about becoming more compassionate to people we encounter who are difficult for us to love and reach out to. The first is about Smith Wigglesworth, one of the most well known healer-evangelists of the last century, and the second is by Brother Yun, a Chinese evangelist who spent years in prison, from his autobiographical work *The Heavenly Man*:

> Wigglesworth was moved with compassion toward the sinner, the sick, the oppressed, the demon-possessed, because he spent so much time in the presence of his Lord that he was like Him.[1]

Brother Yun recorded this story of compassion when he was imprisoned in China for preaching the gospel:

> When I heard this news I immediately felt Huang was a precious soul the Lord had given us to rescue.

> I broke the news to my cell mates and everyone was terrified. They didn't want to receive him. One said, "He is not a man, but a devil." After everyone had voiced their protests I waited for a moment and calmly said, "Brothers, before we believed in Jesus we were just like him. We too were like demons. But Jesus rescued us all when our souls were about to die. We need to have

mercy on this man and treat him as if he was Jesus himself."[2]

Briefly write about each man's approach as it relates to your own life. Can you picture one of these ways as a goal for this season in your life? Which? Write about something that happened when you lacked compassion, but then re-write the experience as you would have liked to respond.

B. Worship

The following statement from the book on Smith Wigglesworth describes worship:

> Very often we try to work up worship, causing it to be very mechanical. True worship comes down into the spirit. From that fountain within, the volume of worship which comes from the very depths of our beings springs forth.[3]

A member of Heart for the World Church wrote this definition of worship:

> A specific act of concentrated submission to God in a setting that is conducive to that submission; using silence, prayer, and music to facilitate an emptying of the mind of clutter and a sloughing-off of our present physical, emotional, and mental concerns in order to make way for a tangible infiltration of the Holy Spirit into our soul, mind, and body.

Describe what worship means to you.

C. Burnout

Here is Brother Yun's description of getting burned out in ministry:

> Because I'd been operating in my own strength for months, I was physically, emotionally and spiritually exhausted. My spiritual eyesight had grown dim and my hearing dull. Pride had sprung up in my heart like a choking weed. Instead of obeying God's voice, I reasoned with human logic and based my decisions on my own wisdom.
>
> My co-workers had warned me not to stay at home, but I didn't heed their advice. I wasn't waiting upon the Lord with a pure heart. This was the root of my failure. I was tired, overworked and backslidden in my heart.
>
> Ministry had become an idol. Working for God had taken the place of loving God. I hid my condition from those who prayed for me and carried on in my own strength, until God decided to intervene in His mercy and love.[4]

Can you relate to any of these statements? Write about a time you were burned out and how you came out of it. How did God intervene? What safeguards do you follow to prevent future burnout? Brother Yun quotes Jesus' warning in Revelation 2:3-5 before describing this period in his life. Look up this passage and journal about its significance in your own life.

OBSTACLES TO WORSHIP

- Not knowing Jesus
- Intellect
- Religious/traditional adversity
- Self-consciousness
- Distractions such as entertainment, life struggles, pursuit of possessions
- Un-confessed sin
- Shame, feeling of unworthiness
- Performance/religiosity
- Self-worship, self-glory
- Demonic strongholds

Here are some helps for worship:

Approach God with freedom –

- to express your true heart in worship and not be forced into a mold;
- to be like a child again;
- from preoccupation with self (and focus on Jesus);
- from the enemy's strongholds that bind us;
- to offer up to the Lord what you're ashamed of.

Try worshiping alone at home with a favorite worship CD.

Be confident – expect a revelation of the Father's heart of love.

What other attitudes and practices can you think of that will help you worship?

OBSTACLES TO COMPASSION

Here are some obstacles to compassion. Which one troubles you the most? Form a prayer asking God to help you overcome it.

1. Old-fashioned selfishness

- What's yours is mine (from hurt and self-pity)
- Nobody cares for me/what has God done for me lately (demanding spirit)
- What's mine is mine and you're not going to get it
- A life focused on getting our spiritual needs met (fostered by popular Christianity)
- Rationalization/excuses/desensitization

2. Not feeling loved, forgiven or accepted yourself (especially by God)

3. Comfortable complacency

- Avoiding exposure to needs of others

4. Religious blinders

- Traditions and distractions cause us to lose sight of people's needs

5. Resentment / un-forgiveness

- Critical spirit: get a job; it's your fault

6. Pride/disdain

7. Fear of being used by people

- I've been hurt before

8. Sense of a lack of resources/abilities

9. Trying to serve under our own power/ performing to impress

10. Lack of faith

11. Compassion fatigue/overload

12. Not knowing Jesus as our savior

Some antidotes to compassion obstacles are:

1. Get a vision of the harvest.

2. Really understand who Christ is in us (Gal. 2:20; Phil. 2:5-8).

3. Remember your mission (take Christ to people).

4. Take responsibility (at least pray).

5. Don't let your work for God crowd out the work of God in you.

6. Act your way into feeling instead of feeling your way into acting.

Can you think of some other ways to renew compassion?

THINGS TO DO

1. Renew your vows with Jesus; get cleansed of any sin or attitudes that stand in the way of God using you.

2. Pray for an awakening of your calling, a vision of what He wants you to do in the Kingdom.

3. Pray for guidance and wisdom to lead you in His plan for you.

4. Fast a meal, two meals, a day or more, in order to draw closer to God. (Fasting also helps you to relate to those who are suffering.)

5. Get your feet wet:

   - Sign up for an outreach
   - Help organize a mini-outreach in your small group circle
   - Get training to go on more extensive mission trips

RECOMMENDED READING

Baker, Rolland and Heidi. *Always Enough: God's Miraculous Provision among the Poorest Children on Earth* (Grand Rapids, MI: Chosen Books, 2003).

Brother Yun. *The Heavenly Man: The Remarkable True Story of Chinese Christian Brother Yun* (Mill Hill, London & Grand Rapids, MI: Monarch Books, 2002).

Manning, Brennan. *The Ragamuffin Gospel* (Sisters, OR: Multnomah Publishers, 2005).

Meyers, Bryant L. *Walking with the Poor: Principles and Practices of Transformational Development* (New York: Orbis Books, 1999).

Mother Teresa. *A Simple Path* (New York: Ballantine Books, 1995).

Pullinger, Jackie. *Chasing the Dragon: One Woman's Struggle against the Darkness of Hong Kong's Drug Dens* (Ventura, CA: Regal Books, 2007).

Ruis, David. *The Justice God is Seeking* (Ventura, CA: Regal Books, 2006).

Sjogren, Steve. *Conspiracy of Kindness: A Unique Approach to Sharing the Love of Jesus* (Ventura, CA: Regal Books, 2007).

Stearns, Richard. *The Hole in Our Gospel* (Nashville, Dallas, Mexico City, Rio de Janeiro, Beijing: Thomas Nelson, 2009).

Walker Tommy. *He Knows My Name: How God Knows Each of Us in an Unspeakably Intimate Way* (Ventura, CA: Regal Books, 2004).

Warren, Kay. *Dangerous Surrender: What Happens When You Say Yes to God* (Grand Rapids, MI: Zondervan, 2007).

NOTES

Chapter Two – Chasing Jesus

1. Wayne Myers with Mary Dunham Faulkner, *Living Beyond the Possible: Trusting God with Your Finances and Your Future* (McLean, VA: Evangeline Press, 2003), 82-84.

2. Ibid., 84.

Chapter Four – Worship and Compassion: The Children

1. "The State of Food Insecurity in the World 2002," Food and Agriculture Organization of the United Nations, http://www. fao.org/docrep/005/y7352e/y7352e03.htm.

2. http://www.wvi.org/wvi/wviweb/nsf/11FBDA878493AC7A 882574CD0074E7FD/$file/Health Annual Report FT08 FINAL. pdf.

Chapter Five – Global Compassion

1. Jim Cymbala with Dean Merrill, *Fresh Wind, Fresh Fire: What Happens When God's Spirit Invades the Heart of His People* (Grand Rapids, MI: Zondervan, 1997), 19.

2. Mother Teresa of Calcutta Center Official Site, http://www. motherteresa.org/layout.html > Mother Teresa>her own words>Something beautiful for God.

Journaling Exercises

1. Albert Hibbert, *Smith Wigglesworth: The Secret of His Power* (Tulsa, OK: Harrison House, 1993), 41.

2. Brother Yun with Paul Hattaway, *The Heavenly Man: The Remarkable True Story of Chinese Christian Brother Yun* (London: Monarch Books, 2002), 142.

3. Albert Hibbert, *Smith Wigglesworth: The Secret of His Power* (Tulsa, OK: Harrison House, 1993), 66.

4. Brother Yun with Paul Hattaway, *The Heavenly Man: The Remarkable True Story of Chinese Christian Brother Yun* (London: Monarch Books, 2002), 198.

CPSIA information can be obtained at www.ICGtesting.com
Printed in the USA
LVOW060409130213

319803LV00001B/15/P